Honoring Parents
in Halachah

A Practical Guide

Rabbi Tzuriel Ta'aseh

Translated by Mordechai Plaut

TARGUM/FELDHEIM

First published 2004
Copyright © 2004 by Targum Press
ISBN 1-56871-334-7

All rights reserved

No part of this publication may be translated, reproduced, stored in a retrieval system, or transmitted in any form or by any means, electronic, mechanical, photocopying, recording, or otherwise, without prior permission in writing from both the copyright holder and the publisher.

Published by:
TARGUM PRESS, INC.
22700 W. Eleven Mile Rd.
Southfield, MI 48034
E-mail: targum@netvision.net.il
Fax: 888-298-9992
www.targum.com

Distributed by:
FELDHEIM PUBLISHERS
208 Airport Executive Park
Nanuet, NY 10954

Printing plates: "Frank," Jerusalem

Printed in Israel

This book is a tribute to our beloved father

MR. GABRIEL CABRA BILDIRICI, *a"h*

who by virtue of his honesty, generosity,
kindness, sincerity, heart of gold, humility,
courage, success, and trust in Hashem
gained the respect and love of the Turkish and
New York communities in which he lived.

לזכר

גבריאל בן ישוע ולאה

בילדיריג׳י הכהן

Gabriel Cabra Bildirici

1923–April 16, 2003

תרפ״ג–י״ד ניסן תשס״ג

RABBI YAAKOV HILLEL
ROSH YESHIVAT
HEVRAT AHAVAT SHALOM
45 ARZEY HABIRA ST. JERUSALEM

יעקב משה הלל
ראש ישיבת
חברת אהבת שלום
רח' ארזי הבירה 45 ירושלים

20 Marheshvan, 5765

APPROBATION

With the greatest of pleasure I looked through both the Hebrew edition and the English translation of this very special and important book, *Honoring Parents in Halachah*, by Rabbi Tzuriel Ta'aseh. The book has already been acclaimed, recommended, appraised, and approved by some of the foremost rabbis of our generation. This new translation into English is certainly a most worthwhile contribution to the community.

I would like to take this opportunity to praise and honor the Bildirici family of New York–Turkey, for making this important book available in English. It is surely befitting that this family, outstanding for honoring their own parents, have undertaken this great mitzvah as a merit for the elevation of the soul of their dear father, Gabriel Bildirici, of blessed memory, and for the benefit of the English-speaking public. I extend my heartfelt blessings to them for success in all their endeavors.

Rabbi Yaakov Hillel

הסכמות

ההסכמות דלהלן נתנו לספר "אוצר כיבוד אב ואם" במתכנתו הרחבה

SHMUEL HALEVI WOSNER	שמואל הלוי ואזנר
RABBI OF	רב אב"ד ור"מ
ZICHRON-MEIR, BNEI-BRAK	זכרון-מאיר, בני-ברק

ב"ה, יום ג' פנחס תשנ"ט לפ"ק

ראה ראיתי ספר יקר ונחמד אוצר דיני כבוד אב ואם מפרי עטו של כבוד הרב הג' מלא ברכת ה' בתורה ויראה צוריאל ב"כ הר' יהודה תעסה שליט"א מפה עיה"ק – והוא אוסף נפלא בהלכות למאות בדיני כבוד או"א בטוב טעם ודעת ונוסף גם כל המקורות ומדרשי חז"ל בעניין זה – לא הניח פינה שלא נשתטח עליו – וניכר שיגע הרבה בתורה וזכה לעשות פירות מתוקים יהי ה' הטוב עמו – ויפוצו מעיינותיו חוצה.

ע"ז בעה"ח - מצפה לרחמי ה'
שמואל הלוי ואזנר

הסכמות

שריה דבליצקי
בני-ברק, רחוב ירושלים 50
טל. 03-6182649

בס"ד, יום ב' אייר תשנ"ט י"ז למב"י

הנה ידידי הנכבד הרה"ג ר' צוריאל תעסה שליט"א מבני ברק בעל המחבר ספר שכל טוב עה"ל מזוזה, הוסיף כעת שנית ידו בחיבור ספר אוצר כבוד אב ואם וכמעשהו בראשונו כן מעשהו בזה, ועוד הגדיל וכו' וראיתי שלא הניח פינה וזוית בהלכות אלה, הכל סידר יפה בעטו, בין חלק ההלכה הפסוקה ובין חלק הביאורים והמקורות והמשא ומתן. על כן מהראוי שהספר הנחמד הזה יודפס בקרוב ויהיה בזה נדבך להגדלת והאדרת הלכה גדולה זאת של כיבוד אב ואם, שכפי שאנחנו רואים צריכה זירוז גדול בקיומה למעשה, ועל ידי ריבוי הספרים והמשא ומתן בזה תגדל גם ההשתוקקות לקיים הלכות אלו על צד היותר טוב, לכל פרטיהן ודקדוקיהן בס"ד. וזכות הרבים יהיה תלוי ונזקף למחבר הנכ' שליט"א. ויזכה עוד להרבות פעלים בחיבור עוד ועוד ספרים נחוצים ומועילים. ובקרוב נזכה לגאולה שלימה בבא"ס ו.

ובאתי עה"ח יום הנ"ל לכבוד כל עמלי תו"י

שריה דבליצקי

הסכמות

משה שטרנבוך
סגן נשיא העדה החרדית בעיה"ק
מח"ס "מועדים וזמנים", "תשובות והנהגות" ועוד
ראב"ד דק"ק חרדים ביוהנסבורג

RABBI MOISHE STERNBUCH
Vice President "Eda Hacharedit"
And Dayan Jerusalem Beth-Din
Head Torah Centre Community
Johannesburg S.A.

הכתובת בירושלים:
רח' משקלוב 13, הר-נוף, ירושלים
טל: 6519610 :TEL

בעזהי"ת, יום ח' אב תשנ"ט

קבלתי הספר "אוצר כיבוד אב ואם" מהרה"ג המופלא הרב צוריאל ב"ר יודא תעסה שליט"א והדברים נפלאים אוצר כפשוטו, והכל בלשון צח וקל שווה לכל נפש, ומעורר כל אחד לקיים המצוה כהלכתה ובהידור.

ואשריו ואשרי חלקו שנתגלגלה לידו זכות כי האי, שיתפשט ויתבדר בס"ד לזכות הרבים, ובזמננו שבעו"ה החופשיים משתדלים בכל כוחם לנתק הבנים מן האבות ששייכים עוד לדור הישן, במצות כיבוד אב ואם מדגישים הדבר "ושאל אביך ויגדך זקניך ויאמרו לך".

ודבריו יתקבלו בס"ד בבי מדרשא, והלומדים ג"כ יפיקו מזה תועלת מרובה, ויש בזה ג"כ חידושים נפלאים, ואלמלא טרדותי בימים אלו הייתי כותב גם דברי תורה אבל עוד חזון למועד. וה' יעזור ויברך אותו ויזכה לחבר עוד ספרים ולזכות הרבים, ובזכות מצות כיבוד אב, שהשווה כבודו לכבוד המקום, ימהר הקב"ה שהוא אבינו שבשמים ויחיש גאולתנו ובמהרה נזכה לקבל פני משיח צדקנו.

הנני המצפה בכליון ממש לרחמי שמים מרובים

משה שטרנבוך

הסכמות

יוסף בן יעקב צוביר

הרב הראשי ליהודי תימן בתל אביב-יפו והסביבה

שע"י הרבנות הראשית והמועצה הדתית לת"א-יפו והמחוז

רחוב גוש עציון מס' 40, תל אביב 67727

יום ראשון י' באלול תשנ"ט

הוגש לפני, למראה עיני, ספר בשם **אוצר דיני כיבוד אב ואם**, מאת המחבר הרה"ג **צוריאל ב"ר יהודה תעסה** שליט"א, כשמו כן הוא **אוצר יקר**, אשר אסף וחיבר איש טהור, מכל המקורות של חכמינו ז"ל, ומספרי הפוסקים והמחברים, המדברים על מצות כיבוד הורים, בודאי שהרב המחבר, זכה זכות גדולה בזה באשר הוא מזכה את הרבים לקיים מצוה כה רבה האמורה בעשרת הדברות **כבד את אביך ואת אמך**, שכן יזכו הבנים והבנות לקיים מצוה גדולה זו מתוך הכרה בכל סעיפיה והלכותיה.

וזכות הרב המחבר תאיר דרכם בקיומה, וכן יזכה ברוב עוז להגדיל תורה ולהאדירה, תוך בריאות איתנה ונהורא מעלייא אכי"ר.

כ"ד המברך בכל לב, הצב"י

יוסף בן יעקב צוביר

תפילת בנים על אבות

רִבּוֹן כָּל הָעוֹלָמִים, יְהִי רָצוֹן מִלְּפָנֶיךָ אֵל רַחוּם וְחַנּוּן, שֶׁתְּזַכֵּנוּ לְקַיֵּם אֶת הַתּוֹרָה וְהַמִּצְווֹת בְּשִׂמְחָה רַבָּה בְּלֵב שָׁלֵם וּבְנֶפֶשׁ חֲפֵצָה וְכֵן נִזְכֶּה לְקַיֵּם מִצְוַת כִּבּוּד אָב וָאֵם בְּשִׂמְחָה רַבָּה וּמִצְוַת מוֹרָא אָב וָאֵם.

אָנָּא מֶלֶךְ רַחוּם וְחַנּוּן, תֵּן בְּלִבֵּנוּ לִשְׁמֹעַ בְּקוֹל אָבִינוּ וְאִמֵּנוּ וְנִזְכֶּה לְכַבֵּד אוֹתָם תָּמִיד, כְּפִי רְצוֹן הַתּוֹרָה הַקְּדוֹשָׁה, וְנֹאהַב אוֹתָם בְּכָל לִבֵּנוּ וְנַפְשֵׁנוּ וְנִהְיֶה אֲהוּבִים לְמַטָּה וְנֶחְמָדִים לְמַעְלָה וּמְמֻלָּאִים בַּתּוֹרָה וּבַחָכְמָה וּבְיִרְאַת שָׁמַיִם.

וְתִזְכֶּה בְּרַחֲמֶיךָ הָרַבִּים אֶת אָבִינוּ וְאִמֵּנוּ שֶׁיִּהְיוּ שְׂמֵחִים בָּנוּ תָּמִיד וְתַצִּילֵם מִכָּל צָרָה וְצוּקָה וְתִשְׁלַח בְּרָכָה רְוָחָה וְהַצְלָחָה בְּכָל מַעֲשֵׂי יְדֵיהֶם וְיִזְכּוּ לִרְווֹת מֵאִתָּנוּ נַחַת דִּקְדֻשָּׁה וּלְגַדֵּל אוֹתָנוּ לְתוֹרָה וּלְמַעֲשִׂים טוֹבִים וְיִזְכּוּ לְאֹרֶךְ יָמִים וּשְׁנוֹת חַיִּים, אָמֵן כֵּן יְהִי רָצוֹן.

עֲשֵׂה לְמַעַן רַחֲמֶיךָ הָרַבִּים וּלְמַעַן אֲבוֹתֵינוּ הַקְּדוֹשִׁים: אַבְרָהָם, יִצְחָק וְיִשְׂרָאֵל עֲבָדֶיךָ. וּלְמַעַן מֹשֶׁה וְאַהֲרֹן, יוֹסֵף וְדָוִד וּלְמַעַן כָּל הַצַּדִּיקִים וְהַחֲסִידִים זְכוּתָם תָּגֵן עָלֵינוּ, אָמֵן.

יִהְיוּ לְרָצוֹן אִמְרֵי פִי וְהֶגְיוֹן לִבִּי לְפָנֶיךָ יְיָ צוּרִי וְגוֹאֲלִי.

Prayer to Be Said by Children

Master of the universe, may it be Your will that we fulfill all Torah and mitzvot with great joy, with a full heart and with an eager soul and that we also fulfill the mitzvah of *kibbud av va'em* with great joy as well as the mitzvah of being in awe of our fathers and mothers.

Please, our King Who is merciful and kind, may we always hearken to our parents and may we always honor them as the holy Torah commands, and may we love them with all our hearts and all our souls. May we be beloved below and cherished Above and replete with Torah, wisdom, and *yirat Shamayim*.

May our fathers and mothers always be happy with us. Preserve them from all trouble and travail and send them blessing and ease and success in all that they do. May they merit to reap holy *nachat* from us and raise us to Torah and good deeds. May they merit long days and lively years. Amen, may it be Your will.

Please do this for Your great mercy, and in the merit of our holy forefathers: Avraham, Yitzchak, and Yisrael, Your servants. And also in the merit of Moshe, Aharon, Yosef, and David and in the merit of all the tzaddikim and *chassidim*. May their merit protect us, Amen.

Contents

Preface 15
Author's Note 17

Chapter 1
The Mitzvah of *Kibbud Av Va'Em* and Being in Awe of Them . . 19

Chapter 2
The Laws of Being in Awe of One's Father and Mother . . . 28

Chapter 3
The Laws of Honoring One's Father and Mother 43

Chapter 4
The Mitzvah of Standing Up for Parents 52

Chapter 5
Expenses Incurred for *Kibbud Av Va'Em* 60

Chapter 6
Being Careful in the Details of the Laws of *Kibbud* 66

Chapter 7
Honoring Parents Who Do Not Keep Torah and Mitzvot . . 72

Chapter 8
When One Should Not Heed His Parents 78

Chapter 9
　If a Parent Waives His Honor. 89

Chapter 10
　Laws of Precedence in Honoring Parents 93

Chapter 11
　Kibbud Av Va'Em in the Context of Other Mitzvot 97

Chapter 12
　Laws of Striking or Cursing a Parent. 103

Chapter 13
　Honoring Other Relatives. 106

Chapter 14
　Honoring Parents after Their Passing 114

　Midrashim and Mussar Sayings on Kibbud Av Va'Em 135
　Stories about Gedolei Yisrael and Kibbud Av Va'Em. 156

Preface

This book is dedicated in memory of our beloved father, Gabriel ben Leah, *a"h*, who passed away on 14 Nissan 5763. Since our father had a very serious accident in 1985, we never took his being alive for granted. We are very thankful to Hashem that He blessed us with our father's presence for many years well into our adulthood.

What is a father? A father is the rock, the security, of a family. Since both of our parents lost their own fathers at an early age, they emphasized the importance of a father in a household and of the respect due to him. Having grown up in Turkey, we learned about the importance of honoring parents and the elderly firsthand.

In Turkey, the way a simple person honors his parents is beyond the imagination of a Westerner of today. In secular Western society, honoring parents has become archaic. Judaism, however, views honoring one's father and mother as a very serious mitzvah, one of the Ten Commandments. Not only that, it is one of the few commandments for which the Torah reveals the reward:

"Honor your father and your mother so that your days will be prolonged."

For those of you who have a father, may we suggest that you take advantage of fulfilling this mitzvah to its fullest extent. When your father asks even for something as simple as a glass of water, you should know that you are fulfilling a positive commandment from the Torah. You should know that Hashem compares the respect due to your father or mother to respect that is due to Him.

We can no longer perform the mitzvah of honoring our father in his lifetime. However, we will continue to honor him and his memory with this book, acts of *chesed*, and *tzedakah*. By these means and others, we pray that Hashem will grant an *aliyah* for his *neshamah*.

We would like to take this opportunity to express our gratitude toward the author of this work, Rabbi Tzuriel Ta'aseh, for allowing us to publish his *sefer* in English. We would also like to thank Rabbi Mordechai Plaut for his expert translation and Rabbi Yehonatan Peretz for coordinating the project.

We are very grateful to Hashem that our mother is still alive and we can perform the mitzvah of honoring our mother. May Hashem bless our mother with many years of health, happiness, and prosperity.

Charlie, Josef, Morris, David, and Nesim Bildirici

Tishrei 5763

Author's Note

Though the halachot in this *sefer* are based purely on the works of the *poskim*, and I have not added any of my own ideas, readers should not rely on this work if doubts arise. Many times the issues are very complicated, and the final decision of the *din* may be determined according to the understanding of the *posek* taking several factors into consideration. In such cases, one should ask a *rav*.

Generally the masculine gender is used in listing the halachot, but most of the obligations apply equally to sons and daughters, as well as with regard to both fathers and mothers.

Chapter 1

The Mitzvah of Kibbud Av Va'Em and Being in Awe of Them

Kabeid et avicha v'et imecha... — Honor your father and your mother, so that your days upon the earth that Hashem your God gives you will be long.
— *Shemot* 20:12

Honor your father and your mother as Hashem your God has commanded you, so that your days will be long and so that it will be good for you, upon the earth that Hashem your God gives you.
— *Devarim* 5:16

❋ ❋ ❋

A man must be in awe of his mother and his father, and you must keep My Shabbat; I am Hashem your God.
— *Vayikra* 19:3

1. It is a positive commandment to honor one's father and mother, and one must be in awe of them. One

must be very careful about honoring and fearing them, since the honor and awe of them is compared to the honor and fear of Hashem. This is among the most serious mitzvot, and it has no limits.

2. The roots of this mitzvah stem from the fact that one must recognize the great benefit one's parents gave him by bringing him into the world, and he must recognize the effort they put into raising him and feel gratitude for this. From gratitude to his parents he will come to feel gratitude toward Hashem, blessed be He.

Also, one who honors his parents strengthens the tradition we have received from our forefathers, transmitted from father to son and stretching back to Mount Sinai, where we were given the Torah from Hashem. One who honors his parents also thereby completes the *tikkun* (rectification) required by his body and soul.

3. The obligation to honor one's father and mother encompasses one's thoughts, speech, and deeds. (The details of each of these will be explained later.) The most important and essential honor is in one's heart: to value one's parents.

4. Some consider the mitzvah of *kibbud av va'em* to be primarily an obligation to Hashem. Others consider it primarily an obligation to the parents. The main consequence of these different opinions is if one is lax in fulfilling his obligations. Should he ask forgiveness of Hashem or of his parents?

The proper procedure is that one who is lax or has transgressed in his obligations to his parents should ask them for forgiveness, but only with regard to the specific, personal obligations of this mitzvah, such as rising for them, and not for indirect obligations that lead to the primary obligations, as will be explained below (paragraph 7; chapter 3, paragraphs 14–17).

5. Whenever one is involved in fulfilling the mitzvah of *kibbud av va'em*, it is proper to have in mind that one is thereby fulfilling the command of Hashem, as is true of all mitzvot — one should fulfill them with the intention of fulfilling a mitzvah of Hashem.

6. As is the case with all mitzvot, it is preferable to fulfill the mitzvah of *kibbud av va'em* personally and not through a *shaliach*, the agency of someone else. Even if one is an important and prestigious person, and even if he is a *talmid chacham*, he should try to fulfill the mitzvah personally.

    However, when it is necessary, it is permissible to honor one's parents through an agent — unless the parents specifically want him to personally carry out those deeds. If so, then he must personally perform the services for his parents.

    Whenever the parents ask a child for something, it is a mitzvah to do it quickly, without any delay.

7. The rule that it is preferable to fulfill the mitzvah personally applies only to direct personal service, such as

giving them food. With regard to indirect services, such as doing their shopping, it depends: if the parents know and are pleased with the fact that their child does the shopping himself, then this is considered direct *kibbud*, and it is preferable if he does it himself. If they will not know whether their child does this service personally, then he can get someone else to do it.

8. It is a mitzvah for parents to educate their children in the laws of honor and awe (such as rising for them, not sitting in their places, and others that will be explained below, in chapters 2 and 3) when the children are young. Since it is necessary to accustom them to perform these important mitzvot, it is not proper that parents should waive these requirements for small children.

9. For various reasons, we do not make a *berachah* when performing *kibbud av va'em*.

10. The mitzvah of *kibbud av va'em* applies even if the parents were not at all involved in raising their children.

11. The mitzvah of *kibbud av va'em* applies even if the parents are strict and demanding. However, if the parents are very difficult people and constantly cause their child distress, he should move away from them. It is always proper in such cases to seek competent halachic guidance.

12. One must fulfill the mitzvah of *kibbud av va'em* even if it causes pain and a lot of trouble to the children.

However, one is not required to get sick as a result of fulfilling the mitzvah.

13. The *beit din* cannot force a person to fulfill the mitzvah of *kibbud av va'em*, since it is a positive commandment whose reward is specified in the Torah, and all such mitzvot are not subject to the compulsion of a *beit din*. However, some say that although *beit din* is not obligated to force a recalcitrant child, it may do so. All agree that everyone should try to persuade a child to honor his parents.

14. Nonetheless, if the parent is suffering disgrace due to the rebellious child, then we compel the child to stop or refrain from such behavior if he is able to do so.

15. One who has sinned against his parents should quickly admit his wrongdoing and ask them for forgiveness. On the eve of Yom Kippur, before going to the synagogue, one should kiss the hand of his father and mother and ask them for general forgiveness.

16. If one took money from his parents without permission, he must return it or ask them explicitly to forgive him. It is even proper to ask them to forgive him if he used money they gave him for a different purpose than they intended.

17. If one sinned against his parents while young, it is good for him to accept upon himself some act to atone for this sin when he becomes an adult.

18. One who fulfills the mitzvah of *kibbud av va'em* prop-

erly merits a long life in this world and in the next. He also merits success, and the Divine Presence will rest on him.

19. Just as the reward for this mitzvah is great, so is the punishment. One who brings pain to his father or mother distances the Divine Presence from himself and causes terrible decrees to descend upon himself and suffers punishments. Even if he appears to be enjoying a good life, payment will be exacted from him in the World to Come.

Who Is Obligated?

20. The rule in the mitzvah of *kibbud av va'em* is that there is no difference between the obligations of a son and those of a daughter, unless she is married (see paragraphs 28–36 below). There is also no difference between the obligation to a father and the obligation to a mother. The Torah says explicitly that the same obligations apply, both with regard to honor and with regard to awe.

A Convert

21. A convert to Judaism may not curse his father who has not converted, and he may not hit him or disgrace him. He should render him a limited *kibbud*.

22. The limits of the *kibbud* are given in accordance with the rule that he should not appear ungrateful to his parents for what they did for him. The specific application of this rule varies with the circumstances and

how his actions are perceived. One should consult a competent halachic authority in such a case.

23. A convert whose non-Jewish parents are sick may pray that they recover.

24. A convert whose non-Jewish parents ask him to visit them along with his children should seek competent halachic guidance regarding the specific circumstances of his case.

25. A convert whose parents converted along with him is not technically obligated in *kibbud av va'em*, but he should render his parents minimal *kibbud*.

An Orphan

26. An orphan who never saw his parents should honor his grandparents when he comes of age. He should take special care to respect and show awe for his teachers and *chachamim,* and he should encourage others to honor their parents and take them to task when they do not do so. In this way, it will be considered as if he honored his own parents. Aside from all this, he should be careful to fulfill all the obligations of honor to his departed parents.

27. An adopted child is not bound to his adoptive parents by the rules of *kibbud av va'em* that apply to a real parent, but he must recognize and give his adoptive parents respect for the kindness they have shown him and continue to show him.

A Married Woman

28. A married woman's obligations in *kibbud av va'em* are limited by the fact that she has an obligation to take care of her husband's affairs.

29. A married woman is released from fulfilling her obligations for *kibbud av va'em* only if her husband minds her doing so. If he does not mind, she must do everything that is practical for her to do.

30. Even though a married woman is not obligated to perform services required in the obligations to honor her parents (see chapter 3), she is not free of the obligations regarding awe. Therefore, she must be careful of the requirements to show awe (see chapter 2), such as not sitting in her parents' places, not contradicting what they say, not calling them by name, and all the other details of these obligations. She is, however, released from those aspects of awe that interfere with her obligations to her husband, such as if her parents ask her to do something but her husband is against it. In that case, she must listen to her husband.

31. A married woman is exempt from *kibbud av va'em* even if her husband is a *rasha*.

32. A woman who is married to the younger brother of her father must still listen to her husband if he does not want her to do something her father asks of her. This is true even though her husband must honor her father, since a man must honor his older brother.

33. If a woman is within the year of mourning for one of her parents, and her husband asks her to attend a public dinner to benefit the synagogue, she may go if her refusal risks upsetting *shalom bayit*.

34. One should not ask something of his married daughter while she is engaged in fulfilling her husband's needs. Nonetheless, her husband should direct her to take care of her father first. Similarly, even if her father is a guest in her home, she should serve her husband first. However, it is proper that her husband tell her to serve her father first.

35. If fulfilling *kibbud av va'em* upsets the *shalom bayit* in his home, a man is also not obligated to fulfill it personally. The reason is that one's obligation to *kibbud av va'em* only involves using the parents' resources. One is not obligated to use *his own* resources, and there is no greater loss than the loss of one's wife. Still, the son should make every effort to convince his wife to allow him to honor his parents. If she nonetheless refuses, he must make every effort to attend to his parents through an agent.

36. A divorced woman has the full obligations of honoring and being in awe of her parents.

Chapter 2

The Laws of Being in Awe of One's Father and Mother

Ish imo v'aviv tira'u — A man must be in awe of his mother and his father, and you must keep My Shabbat; I am Hashem your God.

— *Vayikra* 19:3

The Rabbis learned: What is awe [of one's parent]? Awe means not standing in his place, not sitting in his place, not contradicting what he says, and not determining whether he is correct.

— *Kiddushin* 31b

❊ ❊ ❊

An adult, even if he is mature and independent, remains obligated in every way to honor and be in awe of his parents. The Torah uses the word "ish" when speaking of the obligations of a son to his parents (*Vayikra* 19:3) to teach you that even when one has grown up and married and set up his own household, he should not think that he is free of kibbud av va'em and that he should dedicate himself to his own household. Everyone, young and old, *is obligated to honor his parents and to be in awe of them.*

— Ktav Sofer

1. It is a mitzvah to be in awe of one's father and mother. Practically, this means one should conduct oneself toward them as he conducts himself with someone who can punish him severely, such as a king. He should walk with them as he would walk with someone he fears because he is anxious that nothing happen that the other person dislikes. This is what the Torah means when it says, "A man must be in awe of his mother and his father."

2. "What is awe [of one's parent]? Awe means not standing in his place, not sitting in his place, not contradicting what he says, not determining whether he is correct, not calling him by his name, not speaking authoritatively in his parent's presence, not interrupting his parent, and not flouting what his parent says." This will be elaborated on in the next several paragraphs.

3. How far does the obligation of awe extend? Even to a situation in which the son is dressed in formal clothing and is sitting at the head of his community, and his father or mother comes and tears his clothing and hits him on the head and spits in his face. He must not embarrass them, but should be silent and fear the King of kings Who commanded him to act this way.

4. Some say that anyone who violates the commandment to be in awe of his parents also, necessarily, violates the commandment to honor them. Similarly, anyone who violates the commandment to honor his parents also violates the commandment to be in awe of them.

Standing and Sitting in a Parent's Place

5. One may not stand in a place reserved for his parent, such as a place his father uses when consulting with his own friends. Also, a man should not stand in a place reserved for his father to pray, and a daughter should not stand in a place reserved for her mother to pray.

6. One may stand in a place reserved for his parent to sit, and he may stand on a chair reserved for his parent in order to take something down.

7. One may not sit in a seat reserved for his parent in the home, nor in a seat reserved for his father in the *beit knesset* or *beit midrash*. If, for example, one's father gives a regular lecture and he goes to substitute for his father, he should not sit in the exact place usually used by his father. He should sit somewhere else, or at least move the table or chair slightly from its regular spot.

8. Some say that one may sit in the place in which his father or mother works at home or in a place of business. Others say that this is also forbidden.

The Laws of Being in Awe of One's Father and Mother

9. Some say that all these prohibitions against sitting or standing in a parent's place apply only in the presence of the parent, or at least in the presence of others. Thus, when the child is entirely alone, he may sit in his parent's place. Others say that it is always prohibited, and this is the main opinion.

10. If one's father has a regular seat in the *beit knesset* for *shacharit*, one should not sit there even for *minchah* and *ma'ariv*.

11. If one's father changes his regular seat, one may sit in the old seat. If his father changes to an entirely different *beit knesset*, the son may sit in his father's seat in the first *beit knesset*.

12. Some say that one may not sleep on his father's bed, and some say that he may sleep there, even in the presence of his father.

13. One may sit in his father's place after his father passes away. It is even considered an honor for the father that his son inherit his place.

14. If there is a special chair that is designated for one's parent (meaning that it is different from the other chairs in the household and is recognizably more important), one may not sit in it, even if it is not in the location where the parent usually sits in it.

    A son may wear his father's clothing, and a daughter may wear her mother's clothing, even if they are special clothes. Some say it is better that they do not wear the parents' clothes.

15. One should not pray within four *amot* of his father. However, in a *beit knesset* where there are regular seats, one may sit next to his father to pray.

16. Some write that one should not stand up to take leave of his father until the father gives him permission to do so.

17. If a father and son are at a dinner at which there are guests, or at a meeting or get-together, the son should not sit next to his father. But at home or at the *beit knesset* it is permissible.

Contradicting a Parent

18. One may not contradict his father, whether in Torah or in mundane affairs, as will be explained. If his father has a particular opinion, his son should not nullify his father's position with questions that expose his father's error. Similarly, in mundane matters — for example, if his father is telling a story — the son should not say, "That is not what happened." If the father expresses a particular opinion, the son should not say the opposite.

19. One may differ with his father in a *pesak halachah* when he is not in his father's presence if he has strong proofs that the correct halachah is as he says and the son is an accomplished *talmid chacham*. If he is so wise that he may even differ with his father over a matter of pure reasoning, then he may do so when he is not in his father's presence.

In mundane affairs, one is not prohibited from differing with his father unless he does so in an uncompromising, categorical way. But if he shows his father that the truth is not as the father thought and explains his mistake, then it is not considered as if he is contradicting his father and it is permitted.

20. One may dispute with his father in the course of learning and give-and-take discussions. One may also question, answer, and draw halachic conclusions in the course of such discussions. This is not considered contradicting one's father.

21. Even if the conditions are met for a son arguing with his father (that is, with proof when not in his presence or as part of a learning discussion in his presence), the son must do so with respect and humility and not in a spirit of competition and a struggle for intellectual conquest.

22. If a father is pointing out to his son a mistake he believes his son made, and the son wishes to justify his behavior, he should not directly contradict his father, for example, by saying, "That is not true" or "That's not right." The son should use a less direct approach, saying only that he can justify himself, and then explain the facts as he sees them. Similarly, if the father has asked his son to check his work, for example, and the son finds a mistake, he should not say directly, "Father, you made a mistake," but, rather, "Father, I found a mistake here."

23. Among the laws of awe is a requirement that one should not speak in his father's presence without his father's permission. For example, if they are at a *simchah,* and it is his father's turn to speak, one should not speak in his stead. Even more, if the father is asked a question, the son should not rush to answer before his father does.

24. One should not interrupt his father while he is talking. It should be noted that one who interrupts anyone is considered a boor (see *Pirkei Avot* 5:7).

25. A consequence of the law that one should not contradict a parent is the requirement to obey one's parents even with regard to matters in which the parents have no direct interest and which affect only the child. However, if the child will suffer a loss, or if it affects domestic harmony, or if it causes the child pain, the child is not required to obey his parents when it does not affect them.

26. The prohibition against differing with a parent applies in writing as well, as do the circumstances in which one is permitted to differ. If a son differs with his father, and there is someone else who has taken the father's position, the son should not say his father holds the opposing position when he writes about his own position and argues for it; he should mention the other person.

27. If one's father and another person are on different sides of a controversy, one should not even say that

The Laws of Being in Awe of One's Father and Mother

his father is correct. Doing so slights his father, since it gives the impression that his determination is more weighty than his father's opinion. He certainly should not say that the other side seems correct, since that would be a case of contradicting his father.

Using a Parent's Personal Name

28. Children must not refer to their parents by name, whether during their lifetimes or after they have passed away. One who calls one of his parents by his or her personal name violates a Torah prohibition.

29. The Chida rules that one may refer to a parent by name — whether in his presence or not — if he adds a title to the name, for example, "my honored father... " or "my father, my master... " or "*avi mori...* " or something similar. Sephardim may rely on the ruling of the Chida.

   The Maharshal rules that it is not permitted to use one's parents' names in any case. It is proper that everyone be more stringent in the parent's presence and not use his or her name in such a case, even after adding an honorific title.

30. According to those who rule that one may use a parent's name if a title is added, it does not matter if the title is added before or after the name itself.

31. According to those who rule that one may use the parent's name if a title is added, it is enough to preface the name with "my father" (for example, "my father,

Moshe"). The title father, in addition to implying that he is the biological parent, also connotes importance and a masterly status. He may also refer to his father as "Rabbi So-and-so." Some say that it is even enough if he says that he is the son of So-and-so.

Some say that if one is speaking in public he must say explicitly "*avi mori* — my father, my teacher," and it is not enough to say just "my father."

It is preferable to always say "my father, my teacher, So-and-so" and, similarly, "*imi morati*... — my mother, my teacher, So-and-so."

32. According to those who rule that one may use a parent's name if a title is added, one may refer to his parents as "Grandpa So-and-so" or "Grandma So-and-so." For example, he may tell his children, "We are going to Grandpa So-and-so or to Grandma So-and-so."

33. Some say that even when one refers to his father without mentioning his father's name, he should not say just "father" but rather "my father, my teacher."

34. Even according to those who say that he may not say his parents' name at all (as mentioned in paragraph 29) even when adding a title, if there is a pressing reason, he may use their name with the addition of a title. Thus, for example, if he is asked, "Whose son are you?" he may answer that he is the son of Reb So-and-so, or he may answer, "My father's name is So-and-so."

35. If one goes with a parent to an office or a bank or a

clinic or some similar place, and he is asked the names of his parents when he is with them, he may say their name if he adds a title. Similarly, one who is called to the Torah and is asked his name may answer, "So-and-so, the son of my father, my teacher, So-and-so." He may also answer, "The son of Reb So-and-so." He may answer this way even in the presence of his father.

36. In communities where one is called to the Torah using his own name and his father's name, and one is calling people up to the Torah and he must call his father, some say that he may say, *"Ya'amod avi Ploni* — My father, So-and-so, should stand up," or he may say, *"Avi mori Ploni ben Ploni..."* But some say that he should not mention his father's personal name at all, but just say, *"Ya'amod avi mori..."*

37. If one wishes to make a *Mi Shebeirach* for his parents, and they are not present at the time, he may mention their names, saying, "He should bless my father, So-and-so" or "my mother, So-and-so." But in their presence he should not say their personal names; he should refer to them only as "my father" and "my mother."

38. The prohibition against mentioning the name of a parent applies even in writing. Therefore, when writing about them and relating a story or a saying or a custom or deed of theirs, he should not mention them by name. If he must mention their name, he should be sure to include a title.

39. If one sends a letter to his parents or writes a check made out to them, or he must write their names in his account ledgers, he should write their names with a title.

40. If one must sign his name together with the name of his father, he may sign his father's name without any additional title, for example, "Yitzchak ben Avraham." The law is the same if one must fill in his parents' name on a form. But some say that even in such cases he should add a title. Nonetheless, the general custom is to be lenient in this.

41. If someone's name is Abba (a legitimate Hebrew name, but meaning "father"), some say his children should not refer to him as "Abba" (the title). Others say that since the intent is not to call him by his name but by his title, it is permissible. One who is stringent in this will be blessed.

42. If one's mother's name is Mazal Tov, one may wish her "*mazal tov*" on appropriate occasions.

43. In languages such as Hebrew and Yiddish, where there is a distinction between the singular and the plural in the second person, it is common to address an important person in the second person plural rather than the second person singular. (This distinction is not made in English since the second person plural *you* is used in all cases.) Even in a language where there is a distinction, and it is customary to address an important person in the plural, one should address his parent in the (more familiar) singular. However, in communities

The Laws of Being in Awe of One's Father and Mother

where it is customary to address parents in the plural, one should not deviate from the accepted custom.

44. If one's father is also his *rebbe muvhak*, his main Torah teacher, the custom is to refer to him as "Father" or "Abba" and not "Rebbe" or "Teacher."

45. If one is praying for the recovery of his father, he should not use titles or appellations of honor, since when one is addressing God, it is inappropriate to accord honor to someone else. Therefore, he should not say, "Please heal my honored father, So-and-so," but just "Please heal my father, So-and-so." It is even good to say, "Please heal Your servant, my father, So-and-so," and with regard to one's mother, "Your maidservant So-and-so."

46. Where there are established terms, such as those printed in siddurim (in *Yizkor* where it says, *"nishmat avi mori* — the soul of my father, my teacher" and *"nishmat imi morati,"* and similarly in Birkat HaMazon, where it says, *"Harachaman hu yevareich et avi mori"*), some say that one should say these differently and with greater honor. Others say that where there is an established custom one should not change it.

47. One who is saying a mystic formula to benefit his father (for example, a formula against *ayin hara*, evil eye) may use an honorific title when mentioning his father, such as "my father, my honored teacher." But if he can arrange for someone else to say the formula, it is preferable.

48. If one is saying the prayer for the recently departed for his father, he should not say just his father's name. He should say "my father, my teacher, So-and-so." This is not like a prayer in which one does not use titles with his parents' names.

When Others Have the Same Names as One's Parents

49. When one must refer to someone who has the same name as one's father, if it is an unusual name, one should not use it to refer to the other person, whether in his father's presence or not. If it is a common name, he may not use it in his father's presence to refer to the other person. When he is not in his father's presence, he may use it.

    Some are more lenient and say that a common name is permissible to use even in the presence of the parent, and an unusual name is prohibited only in his parent's presence, in which case he can use it if he changes the name somewhat. The general custom is to be lenient and to permit the use of a common name even in the parent's presence, and this is a substantiated position.

50. The Sephardim have a custom to name their children after living grandparents. Therefore, a boy may have the same name as one of his grandfathers or a girl the same name as one of her grandmothers. Unless they have explicit permission from the grandparents, the parents should not call these children by name in the

The Laws of Being in Awe of One's Father and Mother

presence of the grandparents whom they are named after. If the name in question is unusual, the parents must be careful about using the name (without a change) even when not in the presence of the grandparents. Ashkenazim do not name a child after a living person, including a grandparent.

51. This law, regarding children being named after their grandparents, applies only while the grandparents are alive. After the grandparents have passed away, children may be freely called by their name, even if it is an unusual name.

52. Rabbi Yehudah HeChassid wrote in his will that a man should not marry a woman with the same name as his mother, nor should he marry a woman whose father has the same name as him. Some explain that this is due to the possible problem of calling the spouse by the name of the parent in his or her presence.

53. If one's father is called "Yosef," he may call his friend "Yossi," even in his father's presence, even though Yossi is a common nickname or term of endearment for the name Yosef. If his father's name is Yosef and his friend's name is Yosef Chaim (or vice versa), for example, he may call his friend by his full name in his father's presence. However, if the name is an unusual one, he should not use this name unless it is absolutely clear that he does not mean to call his father.

54. If one's father used to be called by a different name when he was young, because it was later changed or

translated into Hebrew, and the father is now generally called by the second name, the child may call someone whose name is like the father's original name, even in the father's presence. Similarly, if the father had two names and is now known only by one of them, one may call someone whose name is like the father's other name.

55. One may read from *Tanach* or rabbinical works in the presence of his father, even if his father's name is mentioned, and even if it is an unusual name, since it is clear that the son is referring to the person in the *sefer* and not the father. However, one should not read any other text out loud in the father's presence in which someone with the same name as his father is mentioned if it is an unusual name, since it may appear that he is referring to his father and he will be slighting his honor. When he is not in his father's presence, and it is clear that he is not referring to his father, he may read the text out loud, even if he will say his father's name and even if it is an unusual name.

56. One may call someone other than his parents, such as his in-laws or adoptive parents, "Dad" or "Abba" or "Mom" or "Ima." But it is proper to refrain from doing so in the presence of one's real parents.

Chapter 3

The Laws of Honoring One's Father and Mother

The Rabbis taught: He must honor him [his father] in life, and he must honor him in death. How must he honor him in life? If he is doing an errand for his father, he should not say, "Send me on my way so I can finish" or "Hurry up because I am in a rush," but he should ask them to do everything for his father.

❊ ❊ ❊

The Rabbis taught: What is awe and what is honor? Honor is feeding, giving to drink, dressing, covering, bringing in, and taking out.

— *Kiddushin* 31b

❊ ❊ ❊

One who causes pain to his parents through his words causes great damage, since he damages the first two letters of the Holy Name. A person should contemplate how many times he has caused pain to his father or mother since his youth or sullied their honor and how many bad angels he has created as a result. Even the

> slightest act against his parents causes damage on the highest spiritual levels, since HaKadosh Baruch Hu compares their honor to His honor.
> — *Taharat HaKodesh*

Honoring One's Parents in Deed

1. *Kibbud av va'em* in deed means feeding one's parents (when necessary), giving them to drink, covering or dressing them, escorting them when they go into the house or when they go out if they need help, and generally serving them as a personal servant serves his master.

2. The mitzvah extends not only to the parents' immediate personal needs, but also includes indirect needs and benefits, such as doing their shopping, running errands for them, or cleaning their house and the like (see chapter 1, paragraph 7).

3. All these aspects of honoring one's parents are obligatory even if they did not ask him to do them. Some say that if his parents ask him to do one of the things mentioned above (such as feed them), and he does not do what they say, in addition to a failure in his obligation to honor them, he has also failed in his obligation to be in awe of them.

The Extent of *Kibbud Av Va'Em*

4. How far does the obligation to honor one's parents extend? Chazal gives an example: A parent takes a

pouch full of gold coins belonging to his son and wants to fling it into the ocean. The son is anxious about his money and wishes to prevent his father from doing this. Nonetheless, he must not embarrass the parent nor even display his displeasure with him. He must certainly not become angry at him. Rather, he should accept the decree of Heaven that bids him to restrain himself and remain silent.

Some say that before his parent has thrown the pouch, the son may take steps to stop him. He should try to speak to his parent and reason with him, talking in a calm and dignified way. If he is unsuccessful in this approach, it is better if he can find someone else to stop his parent physically, but always very respectfully.

Honoring One's Parents in Word and Thought

5. The fifth of the Ten Commandments is "Honor your father and your mother." This means that when speaking with one's parents one should speak calmly, softly, and deferentially, as one would speak to a king or a very powerful leader. This is the straightforward meaning of the commandment, according to *Sefer Chareidim*. Using traditional exegetical rules (in this case, *gezeirah shavah*), the commentators learned the other obligations as well.

6. The Gemara *(Kiddushin* 31a) says that one person may feed his parent delicacies such as quail and nonethe-

less be severely punished for this, if he does it grudgingly or with open resentment. Another person may send his father to mill flour, and doing so may earn him *Olam Haba* if he does so with honor and dignity and explains to him why it is essential that he engage in this work.

7. If one needs something in the city, and he knows he can get it done in the name of his father, even if he knows that he could get it done for himself as well, he should not say, "Take care of this for me." Rather, he should say, "Take care of this for my father," so that his father will have the honor of people doing things for him. One should take advantage of every opportunity that presents itself for him to increase others' respect for his parents.

8. Using one's father's name and prestige to get something done (as described in the previous paragraph) includes things that have nothing to do with his father. One should just mention his father purely to show that the people will take care of what he needs because of his father's prestige. Some say that even if they do not know his father it is good to mention him, because he thereby increases his father's prestige and honor in general.

9. If one knows others will not do what he needs if he mentions his father, he may ask in his own name. It does not enhance his father's prestige in this case to mention him. If he is not sure how effective it will be to use his

father's name, he may do what he deems appropriate.

10. If one can take care of what he needs done without mentioning anyone — either himself or his father — then it is not necessary to mention his father. But some say that even in such a case he should ask that it be done for his father.

11. When one is praying to HaKadosh Baruch Hu, he need not ask Him to answer his prayers in the merit of his father, even if his father is a great person.

12. If a son hears someone else criticizing or vilifying his parent, he should answer sharply and say, "You are lying." But he should not strike the other person. There are some cases in which it is better to remain silent, such as if one knows that a protest on his part will only bring further vilification from the other party.

13. If one is sitting with his father (or rebbe) and he remembers an interesting question or observation, in general he should attribute this interesting remark to his father (or rebbe), saying, for example, "You once observed..." However, if he knows that the father (or rebbe) will be happy to hear about something he thought of himself, he should say the truth, that it was his own idea.

When Parents Do Not Benefit

14. If one's parents want him to do or not to do something that brings no direct benefit to the parents, some say one need not heed what they say — for example, if

they are afraid he will catch cold and they want him to dress warmly. Others say that even in such a case he must heed them. The latter opinion is shared by most authorities in recent generations, and it is the main ruling. Everyone agrees that he does fulfill a mitzvah if he heeds what they say.

15. In a case where one will suffer a loss or it will affect *shalom bayit,* one need not heed his parents if they request something from which they derive no immediate, physical benefit.

16. If the father commands his child to do something or to refrain from doing something that is in the interests of the child, and not the parent, the child should heed his parent's request as long as he does not suffer a loss. This applies even if the father will never find out whether the child did what he asked.

17. If one's father asks him to stop doing something because the father believes it damages his son's health, the son may not defy his father to his face. Even when he is not in his father's presence, but the father will find out about his son's behavior later, he may not defy his father. But if his father will never find out, and if complying with the father's request seriously disturbs the son, it is permitted for the son to do as he wishes. If a medical issue is involved, the son should make sure he will not suffer harm from doing as he wishes; perhaps his father had a special reason for his request.

The Laws of Honoring One's Father and Mother

Other Aspects of Honoring Parents

18. It is a mitzvah to visit one's parents, since it always makes a mother and father very happy to see their children. There are no rules to determine how often a child should visit his parents. It depends on the circumstances.

19. One should try very hard to get a blessing from his father and mother, even when he is independent of them. By doing so, he fulfills the mitzvah of *kibbud av va'em*. Similarly, in communities where it is common practice, it is a mitzvah to kiss their hand when he sees them, especially on Shabbat and *yom tov*.

20. When one hosts his father, he should seat his father in the most honored seat in the house.

21. The custom to name children after their ancestors (such as naming a grandson after his grandfather) is anchored in holy precincts. The central idea is derived from the mitzvah of *kibbud av va'em*. Sephardim name their children after their parents even during the parents' lifetime. Ashkenazim do so only after the parents have passed away.

22. Some communities give the right to name the firstborn child to the father, and some communities give this right to the mother.

23. If one's father is a *rasha*, one should not name his son after him. However, if the father demands that his grandson be named after him, and the name is that of

a righteous person, he may call his son by that name. When giving the name, he should intend to name his son after the righteous person.

24. *Sandaka'ut* — holding a baby during his brit milah — is a great mitzvah. The *sandak* is considered as one who brings incense on the Altar in the Beit HaMikdash. The custom is to honor one of the grandfathers with being *sandak*. Some communities honor the father's father first, and other communities honor the mother's father first. Everyone should follow his custom.

25. One should try to avoid letting his father be *sandak* if the father is a *rasha*. However, if the grandfather insists and the issue causes quarrels, one suggestion is to have another person who is a *ben Torah* hold the legs of the infant during the brit milah. In that way the *ben Torah* is the *sandak*. The best course in such a situation is to consult a competent halachic authority.

26. It is the custom to honor the most prestigious person present with doing public mitzvot, such as the blessing on a cup of wine for leading Birkat HaMazon or an *aliyah* to the Torah. If one is honored with such a mitzvah and his father is present, he should defer to his father unless the father waives the honor.

27. The true honor a child can show to a parent is by doing good deeds and generally being a *yerei Shamayim*. If the child is good, people praise and bless the par-

ents, saying, "Blessed are they who raised a wonderful person like this." If the child behaves badly, *chas v'shalom*, people say, "Cursed are the parents who raised such a horrible child." In that case, his bad deeds cause disgrace to his parents, who are cursed.

Chapter 4

The Mitzvah of Standing Up for Parents

How careful one must be when it comes to the honor of his father and mother! He must not change any custom or practice of his fathers, even when there is no question of a prohibition or an obligation. We see this in the comment of Rabbeinu Bechayei on the verse "...and he named them [the wells] according to the names that his father gave them" (Bereishit 26:18): "Yitzchak did so for the kavod of his father. From the fact that the Torah notes this, it seems that it was considered meritorious of Yitzchak to have done so. This is inspirational and something for us to learn from — not to make any changes from the ways of our fathers. Yitzchak did not even want to change the names of wells; this certainly applies to the ways of one's fathers and customs or mussar ideas they practiced. Perhaps this was the reason Yitzchak's name was never changed, in direct correspondence to what he did, measure for measure."

We see from the rav how careful one must be not to make a change from the ways of his fathers in any matter. Even in giving names to inanimate objects like the wells, Yitzchak did not want to make a change out of kibbud av va'em.

— *Tochachot Chaim*

1. One must stand up to his full height for his father and mother. There is no difference in this obligation between a son and a daughter. Even a married woman is obligated in this mitzvah.

2. Some say that the obligation to rise for one's father and mother is part of the laws of honoring them. Some say that it is also part of the laws of being in awe of them.

3. The obligation to stand up for one's father and mother begins as soon as the child can see them coming. The child must remain standing until he can no longer see them or until they sit in their place or they go into another area (see paragraph 6 below).

4. If one's father is standing at the place he wants to be, one may sit down even if the father remains standing. For example, if the father is called up to the Torah, once he has reached the *bimah* and is standing in front of the *sefer Torah,* the son may sit down. Nonetheless, it is customary in most Sephardic communities that the son remain standing the entire time that the father is called up to the Torah until the father returns to his seat.

Some say that if one's father stops to talk to someone on his way back to his seat, then one may sit down. It is the consensus, however, that if one's father has merely paused to rest on his way back, one may not sit down.

It would seem that whenever one is uncertain if his father has stopped in the new place, or if it is just a temporary rest stop on the way back to his seat, one should ask his father for permission to sit down.

5. The obligation to stand up for a parent applies whether one is sitting and then he sees his father coming or they are sitting together and the father gets up to leave. In the latter case, one must also rise for his father.

6. If a son and a father are in two different areas (that is, two places that are perceived as distinct and separate, such as two different rooms), the son is not obligated to rise for his father. Since in such a case it is generally not evident that the father's presence is the reason for the son's standing up, it has no honorary or complimentary aspect to it. But if it is evident that the son is standing to honor his father, for example, if the father is about to enter the room where the son is, then the son must rise even if his father is still technically in a different area.

7. The raised platform in a *beit knesset* upon which the Torah is read is not considered, for the purpose of determining if one must rise for his father, a separate area. Therefore, if one is sitting on the platform and his father is passing by, one must rise for him.

8. According to Sephardic halachic authorities, one must stand every time he sees his parents, even a hun-

dred times a day. According to the Ashkenazic halachic authorities, a child must stand twice a day: in the morning and in the evening. However, say the Ashkenazic authorities, if there are people present who do not know that one had already risen for his parent that day, he must rise again for the parent.

9. If one asked his parents for permission not to stand for them, and they have granted this permission, he need not stand for them. Therefore, according to the Sephardic authorities, if one lives with his parents (whether he is single or married), he may ask them to waive this honor during the time he lives with them so that he need not rise every time they enter the room. Similarly, if one works with his parent, he may also ask the parent for such a waiver while they are at work (where it could be awkward). Nonetheless, it is proper for the child to acknowledge them, at least a little, by making a standing motion while continuing to sit. This is called "*hiddur*." If the parents object to such a display each time they enter, he need not do *hiddur* either, since "their will is their honor" — doing their will is honoring them.

10. One who is standing to honor a parent should not lean on anything, but if he is sick or elderly, it is permissible.

11. If one sees his parent approaching and one is standing, it is proper to sit and then stand in their honor to fulfill the mitzvah.

12. One who rises for his father or mother and has to leave immediately should preferably sit down again for a short time. If he leaves immediately, it is not evident that he rose in honor of his parent. But if he must go out to use the restroom, he may go out immediately and need not be careful to sit first.

13. If one's father or mother is blind, one must still rise for them. Similarly, if one is blind, he must still stand in honor of his parents.

14. If one hears a parent approaching, he must get up in his parent's honor even if one does not see his parent and the parent does not see the child. This applies if they are in the same area (as explained in paragraph 6).

15. If one's father or mother has Alzheimer's disease and does not recognize his or her child, the child must still rise in the parent's honor.

16. If the father is riding a motorcycle or is sitting on an animal (such as a horse) or something similar, the child must stand up in his honor. One should even behave stringently and stand up for the father if he is driving by in a car and the child seems him from the side. If the son is riding and the father is standing at the side, the son need not rise in his honor.

17. If one is on a public bus and his parent gets on, one must stand up to his full height. If this is not practical, one should at least make a standing motion while continuing to sit. If his parent has no place to sit, he must give up his own place for the parent to sit down.

The Mitzvah of Standing Up for Parents

18. One does not rise for a parent in a restroom or in a bathhouse, even if both are dressed. Some say one should stand for a parent in a bathhouse. In the middle room of the bathhouse, where some are dressed and some are undressed, if both the father and son are dressed, the son should rise for his father. Certainly in the outer room, where everyone is dressed, the son should rise.

19. If one is sitting *shivah,* he need not rise for his father or mother, and he need not even make a standing motion while continuing to sit. Some say that if he wants to take upon himself to stand, he may do so. On Tishah B'Av, when all are mourners but it is over an old tragedy, one should stand for a parent. However, if one is sitting on the ground, it is enough to do *hiddur* (make a standing motion while continuing to sit).

20. If one is working, he must nonetheless rise for his father or mother. Nowadays there is no difference in this with regard between an employee or an independent worker.

21. If one is lying in bed in pajamas, he need not rise for a parent since that would not be honorable.

22. If one is waiting for his turn in a barbershop and his father enters, he must rise to his full height. However, if he is in the barber's chair, and the barber has started giving him his haircut, he need not get up.

23. The obligation to rise in honor of one's father applies even if the father passes before him in the *beit knesset*

when he is saying *Pesukei D'Zimrah* (in *shacharit*) and even while the son is saying the Shema.

24. If one is learning Torah, he must still rise for his parents, whether he is learning by himself or even teaching a group of people. If he teaches a class, and his father is working there and must enter and leave the room where the class is taking place, he should ask his father to waive his obligation to rise so that he will not need to stand up for his father every time he goes in and out. He also need not do *hiddur*.

25. If one is sitting before his *rebbe muvhak*, the teacher from whom he has learned most of what he knows, or before a prominent *rav*, he is not allowed to rise for his father unless the rebbe generally honors the father or has indicated that he does not mind if the son stands for his father. This is relevant when one sits near his rebbe. If he is sitting far away from his rebbe, and standing for his father will not be considered a slight to the rebbe, then he must stand for his father.

26. If one is sitting and holding a *sefer Torah*, he should not stand for his father.

27. All the laws obligating a child to stand for his parents apply whether the parents are young or boors or simple people — that is, even if they are not people who are generally honored by others.

28. If parents know that their children do not fulfill the mitzvah of standing for them, they should try to

avoid obligating their children. For example, if a father must go into the *beit knesset*, and he can easily arrange to enter when everyone is standing anyway, he should do so rather than entering when his sons are sitting and will not stand up for him. On the other hand, if he sees that they relish the mitzvah, it is good to give them opportunities to fulfill it so that they will please their Creator.

29. If the son is his father's rebbe or the son is extraordinarily wise (and therefore has the same halachic category as a *rebbe muvhak*), each one is obligated to stand for the other. Some say that even though the son must stand, he need not personally serve his father's needs unless he waives his own honor. Such a waiver (*mechilah*) applies only in private or in a place where everyone knows his father. If not everyone knows his father, the son's waiver is not effective, and the best thing is for them to stay apart so that neither should slight the other. This is the arrangement the Maharam had with his father.

30. Just as a person must honor his father and mother by rising for them, he must honor them when entering and leaving a room. He must therefore let them pass through the doorway first and he should not go in or out before them.

31. If one is taking a walk with his parent, he should walk to his parent's left and not to his right.

Chapter 5

Expenses Incurred for Kibbud Av Va'Em

Rav Yehudah said in the name of Shmuel: Rabbi Eliezer was asked, "How far does [the obligation of] kibbud av va'em go?" He told them: "Go and see what an idol worshiper did for his father in Ashkelon. His name is Dama ben Netinah. The chachamim wanted to buy a precious stone for the efod [of the kohen gadol] on which he would have made a profit of 600,000. According to Rav Kahana the profit would have been 800,000. However, the key was under his father's head [and his father was sleeping], and he did not bother him."

The next year HaKadosh Baruch Hu rewarded him: a red cow was born in his herd. The wise men of Israel came to him [to buy the red cow]. He told them, "I know that if I asked for all the money in the world you would give it to me [because you need the red cow]. However, I only ask of you the money I gave up previously by honoring my father..."

— *Kiddushin* 31a

Expenses Incurred for Kibbud Av Va'Em

1. If there are expenses involved in *kibbud av va'em,* they must be borne by the parent and not by the child.

2. If the expenses are not derived from the essential mitzvah, but are incurred only because the child wants to make things easier for himself, they must be borne by the child.

3. According to the law in paragraph 2, if one's parents need assistance and one hires someone to go in his stead, the child, not the parents, must pay the agent.

4. Small expenses for *kibbud av va'em,* such as minor postal costs or telephone charges, are the obligation of the child.

5. If one is his parent's heir and must pay off the parent's debts, one can be forced to pay off the debts if the parent left enough assets to cover his debts, whether they are real estate or other assets. It is *middat chassidut*, a practice of the pious, for the children to pay off a parent's debts even if the parent left no assets whatsoever, since the soul of the departed feels anguish if it still has obligations to someone and the children do not pay off its debts. The children may use their *tzedakah* or *ma'aser* money to pay off their parents' debts in this latter instance.

6. Some say that to prevent the suffering of one's father or mother, one should even give away all his money.

7. If the parent can support himself but does not want to work, or if the parent scrimps and therefore lives a

meager existence, one is not obligated to provide for his upkeep. In practice, it is best to consult with a competent authority in such cases.

8. If one used his own resources to pay for his parents' upkeep even though they had assets, after they pass away he may collect the expenses he incurred from their estate.

9. If one wants an elderly but mentally competent parent to move near him so that he can help him properly, but the parent refuses because of the high rent, one may not take money out of the parent's bank account without his permission, unless one has the authorization of a *beit din* or at least the consent of a *gadol*.

10. If elderly or sick parents who cannot support themselves or are mentally incapacitated have resources, the family is allowed to use the parents' resources even without the knowledge of the parents in order to support them and to tend to all their needs with dignity. The family need not borrow the necessary funds and then pay back the debts from the estate. It is proper, in such circumstances, to ask the advice of a rabbi before doing anything.

11. If parents do not have the resources to support themselves, a Jewish *beit din* might force the children to support them. This obligation on the part of the children stems from their obligation to do *tzedakah* (charity) and not from their obligation of *kibbud av va'em*.

12. Even though the basis for the obligation to feed one's parents when they cannot do so themselves is an obligation to do *tzedakah* (as explained in the previous paragraph), one may not suffice with giving the amount he would normally give to any poor person. If he has the means, he must meet his parents' needs generously, beyond his minimal obligation of *tzedakah*. This is the common custom.

13. If one does not have enough to support his needy father unless he lowers his own consumption, he should do so. For example, if the son has enough to buy himself bread and meat, he should not buy himself the meat but instead buy bread for his father. But if he does not have even that much, he is not required to go begging for his father's needs. Still, it is proper to even beg for his father, if he can do so, out of good manners and natural expectations. Under no circumstances should he let his mother go begging.

14. If one has enough to support his needy parents from his own, personal money, he should not use *tzedakah* money to support them. The Rabbis said, "Anyone who gives the tithes for the poor to his father will be cursed" (*Tosefta, Ma'aser Sheini* 4:6). Some say this is prohibited even if the parents do not know that they are receiving charity, but that if the parents do not know, it is permissible to use charity money. However, if one is hard pressed and cannot pay for his parents' needs from his own money, he may use *tzedakah* money without any qualms.

15. If one wants to support his parents from his *ma'aser* money even though he has the means to support them from his general resources, this is permissible under the following circumstances: If every time he gives *ma'aser* he says, "*bli neder*" (that is, that he does not give *ma'aser* as an obligation equivalent to an oath), then he may support his parents from the *ma'aser*, since the money given is not considered *tzedakah* but just plain, voluntary giving. However, if the first time he gave *ma'aser* he did not say "*bli neder*," and his intent was to continue giving *ma'aser* regularly, then he may not support his parents from money set aside as *ma'aser*.

16. In a case where the parents must be supported by their children, the expenses should be apportioned among the children according to their ability to pay. If some children are wealthy and others are poor, then only the wealthy children are obligated to support their parents. Some write that even the personal attention to the needs of the parents is the responsibility of the wealthy children alone.

17. Even though, as mentioned (paragraph 1), expenses involved in *kibbud av va'em* must be borne by the parent and not by the child, one must honor his parents even if it will cause him to miss out on opportunities for profit, for example, if he must neglect his own work in order to attend to the needs of his parents and he will thereby lose out.

18. If one has enough food for the current day, he must forgo his own work in order to fulfill *kibbud av va'em*, including honoring his parents personally, even though by neglecting his own work he may become poor and have to beg for a living. Some say that this rule applies only to someone who has a steady source of daily income through which he can earn his daily needs; however, if he has no regular source of income, and some opportunity arises for him to earn money, he need not forgo his income even if he has enough food for the current day, unless he has a thirty-day supply of food.

19. Even though a child is required to give up his own work in order to honor his parent, this extends only to work he does himself. He is not required, for example, to have his parents live with him for free if he could rent out or sell that part of his home.

20. If a man does not want to support his wife, and the *beit din* cannot force him to support her — say, because he is a violent person — then her son must support her even using his own resources. And certainly, if the father is not obligated to support the mother, then the child is required to support her. This could occur if she is one of those Chazal say is fined (for some transgression), and her husband is therefore not obligated to provide for her.

Chapter 6

Being Careful in the Details of the Laws of Kibbud

Cursed is one who disgraces his father and his mother...
— *Devarim* 27:16

"Makleh aviv — who disgraces his father" means one who slights and disgraces them, similar to "V'niklah achicha l'einecha — And your brother will be disgraced before your eyes."
— *Rashi*, ad loc.

❋ ❋ ❋

If one causes pain to his father and his mother, then HaKadosh Baruch Hu says, "It was good that I decided not to live with them. If I had lived among them, they would have caused Me pain."
— *Kiddushin* 31a

❋ ❋ ❋

An angel of God came and sat under the terebinth tree near Ofra, which belonged to Yo'ash of Avi Ezri. His son Gidon was threshing grain in the winery in order to avoid observation by Midian.
— *Shoftim* 6:11

Being Careful in the Details of the Laws of Kibbud

Gidon said to his father, "Father, you are old. Go home and I will thresh, for if the Midianites come, you will not have the strength to run away." [Observing this] the angel said, "You fulfilled the mitzvah of kibbud av va'em and you are worthy to redeem bnei Yisrael." Immediately the angel of Hashem appeared [to Gidon] and told him, "Hashem is with you, mighty warrior."
— *Radak*, ad loc.

1. One who belittles his father and his mother, or even hints at it, is included among those who are cursed by the Almighty, as it says, "Cursed is one who disgraces his father and his mother" (*Devarim* 27:16). The *beit din* can take steps to punish such behavior, even with lashes.

2. Part of the requirements of *kibbud av va'em* is that it be performed graciously and with a pleasant demeanor. One might bring his father delicacies but as a result lose his share in the World to Come (if he brings him the food grudgingly — *Rashi*). In contrast, one may have his father work at the grindstone, but as a result acquire a share in the World to Come (if he speaks to him softly and explains to him the necessity of doing the work — *Rashi*; see *Kiddushin* 31a–b).

3. Another aspect of honoring one's parents and being in awe of them is being very careful not to cause them any distress, whether actively or passively. Therefore, it is best not to tell them bad news that is not important for them to know, even if it does not affect them

directly. One should also be careful not to stop doing anything they have become used to, since one may thereby cause them distress.

4. If one's parent is critically ill with a terminal disease and the doctors have not told him or her the truth about the condition, even if one's parent commands him to tell him the truth, one should not heed the parent in this.

5. If one's parent has a dangerous condition but refuses to undergo important tests because they involve great pain, one may use subterfuge to have the procedures done even against the parent's will. But if the condition is not a dangerous one, it is not permitted to have medical tests done against the parent's will.

6. If one has a financial claim against his father or mother, according to the letter of the law he may take them to court. Nonetheless, the *beit din* should speak to the son and try to convince him not to take his parents to court.

7. If someone is on trial in the secular court system and believes he can reduce his sentence by arguing in his defense that he suffered as a child from a domineering father who used to beat him, he is not allowed to use this argument, since it demeans his father.

8. Even if one can realize a great profit, he may not cause his father distress in order to do so. That is to say, although one is not required to suffer a loss for *kibbud av*, he is required to forgo a profit. It goes without say-

ing that one may not pressure his parents to give him money for his needs, and if he pleads with them to give him money against their will, he may transgress several Torah prohibitions

9. One may not enter the same business as his father without his father's permission if they are in the same city and will be competition for each other.

10. One should be careful not to undertake voluntary religious behavior if it causes his parents distress. For example, he should not fast voluntarily or immerse himself in an extremely cold *mikveh* if his parents are concerned about the effects these actions will have on his health.

11. If the father is known for his high standards of religious observance, the son should be careful not to pursue leniencies or to belittle mitzvot. He should even be careful to refrain from an act that may involve a rabbinical prohibition, even if it is permissible according to the letter of the law. The reason for this is that if he is not careful in doing mitzvot he will embarrass his father.

12. One may not wake up his father or mother, even if he suffers a loss as a result. However, if one knows that his father will be upset at the loss that was caused by not waking him up, it is a mitzvah to wake up the father.

13. One may wake up a parent if the parent must fulfill a mitzvah whose time will soon pass, such as saying

Shema or *tefillah*. If possible, one should try to find someone else to wake him. If it is a mitzvah that is not critical, such as praying together with a minyan and not privately, he should not wake up his father unless he is certain his father will be happy to have been awakened. Similarly, if a poor person comes to the door for *tzedakah*, one should not wake up his father unless the father left instructions to awaken him if anyone comes to collect money for a mitzvah.

14. In those communities in which it is considered a bigger mitzvah to open the *aron kodesh* to take out the *sefer Torah* than to put the silver ornaments onto the *sefer Torah*, one should not open the *aron kodesh* while his father puts the silver ornaments onto the *sefer Torah*, unless his father gives him permission to do so.

15. If one's father is trying to buy an *aliyah* to the Torah, one may try to outbid him to buy it for himself if he knows that his father does not object.

16. It is not nice for a person to ask his mother or father to serve him in any way, even, for example, to ask them to pass a cup that is near them and even if he knows they do not mind. Similarly, one should not appoint his father as his agent, even if it is for a *devar mitzvah*, such as checking his home for *chametz* before Pesach or separating *challah* from dough or tithing produce.

17. If one does need the help of his mother, he should not give her orders to feed him or to arrange his affairs or to sew his clothing or the like. Rather, he should speak

indirectly, saying, for example, "My coat has torn" or "Is it possible to eat now?" or something similar, as appropriate.

18. If one wants to ask his mother to watch his children, he should not say to her, as if he were ordering her, "Watch the children." Rather, if he is taking his children to her, he should say something like "We are going to So-and-so, and we have brought our children here" (implying that he wants his mother's help, but not saying so explicitly). If one wants his mother to come over to his home to watch the children, he can say something like "We are going to So-and-so. Can you come over to us?"

19. One should not ask his father or mother to prepare him something to eat or drink and the like. If his parents ask him what he wants to eat or drink, he should not say, "Make me such and such" but he should say (indirectly), "Let's eat such and such" or "Let's drink such and such."

20. If one is working with his father, he may say to him, "Give me so-and-so object (needed for work)." Or he may say, "Please take this object."

Chapter 7

Honoring Parents Who Do Not Keep Torah and Mitzvot

Yosef did his father's bidding, and he said, "Here I am," and he went quickly, with enthusiasm, even though he understood that he was going to his death because he knew of his brothers' hatred toward him. With all this, he did not say, "My dear father, they hate me, and who knows what will happen?" Instead, he listened to what his father said, and he fulfilled his father's request even though he was in great danger. And even though Chazal said that if your father tells you to violate Shabbat, you should not heed him because both you and your father are required to honor Hashem [and chillul Shabbat is dishonor of Hashem], this rule applies only where the limitation is an obligation directed to Shamayim. But if it is an issue that affects oneself, one may agree to do the will of his father.

— Shlah, *Derech Chaim, Vayeishev*

1. According to the *Shulchan Aruch*, one must honor his father even if his father does not keep Torah and

mitzvot. However, the Rema says, "Some say he is not obligated to honor his father unless his father does *teshuvah*." But the opinion of some later authorities is that even according to the Rema one should try to follow the opinion of the *Shulchan Aruch*.

2. Even according to the *Shulchan Aruch*, which says one should honor a parent who sins, this refers only to a parent who sins because he cannot control his desires. However, if the parent sins out of principle, like heretics and apostates who are comparable to non-Jews, he certainly may not honor them. This applies even more so if the parents converted to another religion.

3. If one became religious, but his parents do not keep Torah and mitzvot, one may give them the benefit of the doubt and consider them like a baby who was never given a proper chance to keep the Torah. In that case, even if the parents continue in their old ways and, for example, violate Shabbat in public, the children should honor them. In this way, they will increase *kavod Shamayim,* the glory of Heaven, and perhaps the parents will see this and become religious as well, experiencing the pleasant ways of the Torah. But if the parents hate religion and give their children a very hard time, they are like heretics and apostates and certainly should not be honored. In such a case, the best course, if it is possible, is to distance oneself from one's parents and live in another city.

4. Even according to the *Shulchan Aruch,* that one should

honor a parent who is sinful, one should not show honor to them in the specific area where they had sinned. Therefore, if one wants to honor his father by rectifying his parent's sin, he need not do so. For example, children need not return interest their father charged out of respect for their father, even if the amounts are clearly identifiable, unless the father repented of his sin before his death.

5. If one's parents are not observant, and one has tried, unsuccessfully, using gentle persuasion and other nonaggressive methods, to convince the parents to say *berachot* over food and drink that one serves them, the child may continue to serve them (even though one is not permitted in general to give food to a Jew who will not make a *berachah*). The hope is that if one treats his parents with honor and dignity, perhaps his parents will also become observant.

6. One must honor his parents after their death even if they were not observant. He should do whatever is necessary to benefit their souls, even if it is known that they did not repent before they died.

However, if the parents converted from Judaism, the children may not honor them even after they die. He should not rend his garments over their passing, nor sit *shivah*, nor observe the laws and customs of the thirty-day mourning period or the twelve-month mourning period. One also does not say Kaddish for them nor do the other things that are customary to do for departed relatives. (Nonetheless, if the son *wants* to say Kaddish to benefit their souls, he is allowed to do so.) If they were killed, their death atones for their sins, and one should mourn them. One should also mourn them if they confessed their sins and repented before their deaths.

Rebuking a Parent Who Sins

7. If one sees a parent committing a sin — whether in violation of a biblical or rabbinical law — he must point out his parent's error. However, he must not do so in an insulting way or by directly challenging the parent. For example, he must not say, "Father, you have violated a law of the Torah" or "The law is not as you imply, since it says such-and-such in the Torah," or something similar. He should rather use an indirect, questioning approach. For example, he might say, "Father, I see you are doing such-and-such. Was this the Torah's intent? What about the following passage in the Torah?" He should present the issue as if he is in doubt and questioning, not challenging.

8. If one's father is a *talmid chacham* and one sees him committing a sin, one can say, "Father, you taught me such-and-such." Even if one knows his father never actually taught him the point in question, he may speak this way to preserve the honor of his father. If one's father is not familiar with Torah and halachah and his father is committing a sin, he can say, "Once there was a person who did such-and-such, and the *rav* told him that doing so is forbid-

den." Since he expresses it as part of a story, the criticism is hidden and doing so is permitted.

9. If one's parents are *ba'alei teshuvah* who do not know any halachot, and one must teach them many things, he may address them more directly, particularly since they are not ashamed of their lack of knowledge in comparison to their son. However, even in this case one should take care to avoid saying to them, "You have committed a sin," or similar statements. One should show them the right way to do things in a gentle manner.

10. If one sees one's father about to commit a sin, or he sees him in the process of committing a sin, he should preferably use the approach outlined in paragraph 7. However, if the father does not respond, or if the son fears that using that approach will take too long and he will not succeed in preventing his father from sinning, he may say to him clearly and unequivocally that doing this act is forbidden. Still, he should do it gently and with honor and not insult his father, God forbid.

11. If one's father is making a mistake in quoting something from an outside source, one should not say, "Don't say it over that way." Rather, one should say, "Father, this is what we heard" or "Father, this is what we learned," or something similar.

Parents with Impaired Mental Faculties

12. If one's father or mother loses his or her mental faculties, he should try to bear with them until Heaven has mercy upon them and restores their faculties. However, if the condition has deteriorated to the extent that one cannot deal with his parent properly, and sometimes he has to scream or even hit the parent for his benefit, he should go away and arrange for someone else to take care of his parent.

13. If a parent's condition deteriorates to the point that he needs to be physically restrained, one may not do this himself. Rather, he should arrange for someone else to do what is necessary. If the parent is harming himself and there is no one else around, one may restrain the parent himself. The child should make every effort to place his parent in a proper institution where the parent will be well taken care of.

Chapter 8

When One Should Not Heed His Parents

A person should exert himself and try hard to get a berachah from his father and his mother, and even if he does not live in their home but lives far away, he should not be weak and should go every Friday night and Shabbat day and on chagim to kiss their hand and to receive their blessing. Aside from the fact that their berachah is liable to be fulfilled since it comes from them wholeheartedly, as a father feels toward his children (Tehillim 103:13), [going to one's parents] has another virtue: it is a mitzvah for him since he is thereby honoring his father and mother, and he will be rewarded [for it]. The Midrash says that all the goodness and royalty that are enjoyed by the descendants of Esav are the result of the fact that Esav valued the berachah of his father, and he cried out a great and bitter cry when saying, "Father, please bless me as well" (Bereishit 27:34).

— *Pele Yo'etz, Berachot*

1. Since both parent and child must honor Hashem, if one's parent tells one to do something against the To-

rah — whether it is a Torah commandment or based on a rabbinical decree, and whether it is something that relates to a person's relationship with Hashem or to a person's relationship with his fellow — one should not heed the parent. It makes no difference whether the parent is deliberately violating the Torah or not. Included in this principle is that one should see to it that his parent fulfills all his responsibilities to Hashem (if the parent is doing something improper), even if one may not be able to maintain the full level of honor and awe for his parent in doing so.

2. Even if one's parent asks him to refrain from doing a mitzvah that is not obligatory — for example, if one's father tells him not to wear a four-cornered garment so that he will not be obligated to fulfill the mitzvah of tzitzit — the child need not heed his parent. However, if the parent gives a reasonable basis for asking him to refrain from the mitzvah, one must heed him.

3. Even if one's parent asks him to refrain from doing something that enables a mitzvah, the child need not heed his parent. Therefore, if a father objects to his son serving as a *sandak* at a brit milah, and the father does not give a reasonable basis for his objection, it is tantamount to the father telling his son to violate a mitzvah and the son need not heed his father.

4. If one's parent asks him to neglect something that is an aspect of a mitzvah, for example, the mitzvah to do other mitzvot quickly and early or a beautification of

a mitzvah, since the issue is not the essence of the mitzvah itself, one must heed one's parent, as long as the parent gives a good reason for his opposition. For example, if one wants to make a brit milah early in the morning, and his parents ask him to make the brit in the afternoon since they want to allow time for certain guests to come, he must heed their wishes — unless he is able to convince them, possibly by getting a third party to speak with them, to go along with his desire to make the brit early in the morning.

5. Even if one's father asks him not to do something that only *might* constitute neglect of a positive mitzvah, he should not heed him. For example, if one's father asks him not to return an object that may not be lost, or, if it is definitely lost, it may be that the original owner already gave up hope of getting it back before one picked it up. The certain obligation of *kibbud av* does not override even the doubtful obligation to return the object.

6. If one's parent asks him to do something that is contrary to an established *minhag* (custom), one should also not heed the parent, since *minhag Yisrael* is also Torah, and it is considered as if the parent asked the child to violate the Torah itself. This refers only to a *minhag* that everyone does. However, if it is a *minhag* that not everyone does, and one has undertaken to keep it, one should listen to his parent if the parent gives a good reason for his objection. If one has already fulfilled the *minhag* three times, he must go to a *chacham* for *hatarat nedarim* (nullification of vows).

7. If there is some *middat chassidut* that is not mentioned in *Shas* or brought down in the *Shulchan Aruch* that one wishes to follow and his parents object, and they give a reasonable basis for their objection, one must listen to them.

8. If one's parent is not observant, and the parent asks him to bring him food that is forbidden to eat, or to help him do something else prohibited, one should not do it.

9. If one's parent asks him to bring him something that is definitely injurious to the parent's health, one should not do it.

10. If one's parent asks him to do something in the parent's honor that involves danger, one must not endanger himself. However, if one's parent has a life-threatening illness and needs medicine, even if the trip is somewhat dangerous, one may go to bring the medicine for him.

11. If one is a doctor and he is called to help in a place that is vulnerable to terror attacks, and his parents are concerned for his safety and tell him not to go there even to help, one need not heed them if the danger is slight. He should, however, take along his tefillin to help keep him safe.

12. If one keeps his hair short for religious reasons, and his father wants him to let his hair grow longer, one should not listen to his father.

Honoring Parents in Halachah

13. If one's father tells him to cut his beard off, he need not listen to his father. If one is cleanshaven but now wants to grow a beard and *peyot,* and his father protests, one should ask a *rav* who is a *talmid chacham* and *yerei Shamayim,* and who knows him and his family, if this is the proper time to grow a beard and *peyot.*

14. If a young man has very long *peyot* and his father asks him to cut them shorter, saying that they will make it harder for the father to find his son a *shidduch,* the son must listen to his father.

15. If one's parents tell him not to honor his wife, or her parents tell her not to honor her husband, in a specific matter or in general, and in such a way that it will have a deleterious effect on *shalom bayit,* they need not heed their parents.

16. If one's parent is dangerously ill and asks him to leave his wife and family to attend him in the hospital, one must do so even if it upsets *shalom bayit.* Since this may involve *pikuach nefesh,* the wife is also obligated to sacrifice to save her in-law.

17. If a man's parents tell him not to visit his in-laws, he need not heed them.

18. If one wishes to move to Eretz Yisrael to fulfill the mitzvah of settling Eretz Yisrael, and his parents object to his going, he need not listen to them (see chapter 11, paragraph 5).

19. One may leave Eretz Yisrael in order to fulfill the

mitzvah of *kibbud av va'em* as long as he does not plan to settle outside Eretz Yisrael permanently.

20. If a parent tells his adult son to tell people who come looking for the father that he is not at home (even though the father really is at home), the son may say that the father is not home because of *darkei shalom*, to keep the peace.

21. A person should be very careful not to aggravate an unjustified dispute, even if his father is one of the quarreling parties. In such a case, he should be very careful not to honor his father by taking his father's side. Even if his father asks him directly to get involved, he should not.

22. If one's parent told him not to speak to someone and not to forgive the person for something he did, at least until a certain time has elapsed, but one would be willing to forgive and make up right away were it not for his parent's request, one should not take into account his parent's request. Nonetheless, one should act intelligently and not anger his parent to his face by public displays of affection for his parent's rival.

23. If one is a *talmid chacham*, and his father or mother needs some service that requires an act that is very demeaning, and it is probable that he would not do this service for himself, he need not serve his parents in this aspect in public. However, in private he has to do anything for them that is required due to his obligation to honor them.

24. If one's parent asks him to do something silly, he need not heed his parent.

25. If one's father sends him to call his mother for some reason, and the mother is asleep, he should not awaken her.

26. If one wants to pray in a *beit knesset* where the people pray with greater *kavanah* and his father protests, he does not have to listen to his father as long as the matter does not cause a quarrel with his parents.

27. If one's parents ask him to do something that involves *chillul Hashem*, he must not heed their request. For this reason, one may not attend an intermarriage ceremony, *Rachmana litzlan*, even if his parents plead with him to go along with them.

28. Similarly, if one's parents are not observant and they make a birthday party or celebrate their wedding anniversary in a non-kosher restaurant, he may not participate.

29. If one's parents are not observant and do not keep Shabbat, and they want him to spend Shabbat with them in an atmosphere of *chillul Shabbat*, he should not agree. If the parents themselves keep Shabbat, but the place where they are staying has an environment of *chillul Shabbat*, and going there for Shabbat will cause one to suffer just from having to be in such a place for Shabbat, he should not spend Shabbat there, since Shabbat is meant for pleasure, not for suffering.

When One Should Not Heed His Parents

30. If one's mother is ill, and she asks him to drive her (during the week) to his sister to recover there, and one knows that his mother will surely travel back to her own home on Shabbat, he may drive her there if he knows that she will violate Shabbat anyway.

31. If one's father asks him to come to eat *seudah shelishit* (the third Shabbat meal) with him on Shabbat, but the son has not yet prayed *minchah,* and he usually follows the opinions who say that one should not eat *seudah shelishit* before *minchah,* he should still obey his father.

32. If one wants to fast in order to atone for a sin, and his parents are concerned about his health, according to the letter of the law he need not listen to them and he may fast. However, it is appropriate for him to consult a *chacham* as to how he might be able to do *teshuvah* for his transgressions in a completely positive way so that his parents will not object.

33. If one wants to study Torah in a yeshivah all day, and his parents want him to study secular subjects at least part of the day, he need not heed them and interrupt his learning, even if their intention is to provide him with an honest and easy trade or profession.

34. If one feels that he progresses in learning when he studies with a particular person, and his father objects to his studying with that person, he should not listen to his father. However, if the father's objection is based on the fact that the person is not a *yerei*

Shamayim or a similar consideration, then he must obey his father.

35. If one's father tells him that he should not learn in yeshivah until late at night out of concern for his health, the son should heed his father and go to sleep early, because doing so is beneficial both physically and spiritually.

36. If one's father objects to his becoming a *dayan* (judge) and decrees that he should not do so, one need not adhere to the decree.

37. If there was a *machloket* (dispute) about a certain *din* (law), and one's father wishes him to follow the stricter opinion, he must listen to his father if their community generally follows the stricter opinion. But if the father wishes him to follow the lenient opinion, against the accepted practice in their community, he need not listen to his father.

38. If one's father follows a lenient opinion about a particular halachah, and one now wishes to follow a strict opinion but the father objects on the basis that he is concerned about the welfare of his son, or he has another valid reason for his objection, then one must listen to his father. It is proper, in such a case, to consult a *chacham*.

39. If one's father asked him to follow the same halachic authority as the father, and there is no accepted custom in their community, or there are different accepted customs within the same community, or dif-

ferent authorities issued different rulings and one's father follows one authority while one follows a different authority, then it depends: If one's father follows a more lenient authority, one need not listen to him. If the father follows a stricter authority, then it is proper for the son to heed his father's request, as long as doing so does not cause him financial loss or upsets his household.

40. If one's father speaks to him and expects an answer, even if he has already said the *berachah* of *Hamapil* before going to sleep (and one should try not to talk between saying that *berachah* and going to sleep), he should answer his father.

If Parents Oppose Their Child's Marriage

41. Parents do not have any right to object to the marriage of a son or daughter, even if the basis of their objection is that as a result of the marriage the child will move away (thus causing them to lose the honor they are entitled to).

42. If parents object to a proposed marriage of their son because his intended has done things that have earned her a bad reputation, then the son must listen to them. But if she is perfectly suitable to be a wife for the son according to the laws of the Torah, except that the father or mother have some personal dislike of her, or the parents say that according to their understanding she is not a good match for the son, or even if

Honoring Parents in Halachah

the father argues that a girl like her does not fit with their family (for example, if the girl's family is not distinguished enough or if the girl is from a community or ethnic background that the father and his community consider beneath their own community or if members of the girl's family are unsavory characters), the son need not heed his parents.

43. If one wants to marry a woman who has undergone a proper conversion in a *beit din,* but his parents object that having such a woman in the family is beneath their dignity, he need not listen to his parents.

44. Even though, as mentioned above (paragraph 41), parents cannot prevent the marriage of their son or daughter, it is proper for every son and daughter to consult with his or her parents about whom to marry and to give due consideration to their opinion and experience and general impression of the proposal at hand, especially since the parents have their children's best interests at heart and know them well.

45. If one's father tells him to divorce his wife, he is not required to listen to the father. However, if the woman has done things or has behaved in such a way that halachically one should divorce her, then it is a mitzvah for him to listen to his father.

Chapter 9

If a Parent Waives His Honor

> *"In order that your days be lengthened..." (Shemot 20:11) — I am warning you to be careful to honor your parents so that your own days shall be lengthened, and so that you will have sons and daughters. If you honor your father and mother, then your own children will honor you in your old age, since one receives in the same measure as he gives out. Therefore, kibbud av va'em is not just for the elderly who receive the honor, but also for the benefit of the son who honors them, since it is a cycle that always comes around again in the world.*
> — Based on *Abarbanel*

1. If one's father or mother waive their honor (*mechilah*), it is valid. But it is written in *Sefer Chassidim* that there is still a Heavenly obligation to honor them. Recent authorities bring this opinion as halachah.

2. In small matters about which it is common that people are not concerned, the *mechilah* of the parents is effective even with regard to the Heavenly obligation. Also, in a case in which one wishes to serve his parent,

but the parent does not want that service — for example, the parent prefers that his child rest at that time — one will certainly not be punished, since one honors a person by doing his will.

3. Just as parents can waive their child's obligations in the mitzvah of honor, so they can waive the child's obligations in the mitzvah of awe. However, in a situation in which a lack of awe for the parent will cause dishonor for the father or mother, *mechilah* does not take effect. The parents are not able to waive their disgrace or pain, and they certainly may not permit themselves in advance to be hit or cursed.

4. Parents cannot waive their disgrace only when it is the child who is disgracing the parent. However, if the father or the mother want to perform some service for their child that will dishonor them, for example, if they want to wash their son's feet, and doing so will make them happy, it is permitted if the parents truly want to do it very much. However, if the child can convince them not to do this, he should do so and not accept their service.

5. Effective *mechilah* from a parent means an explicit statement of *mechilah*. If they are silent, it should not necessarily be considered a conclusive indication that they have waived their honor. But if the circumstances indicate conclusively that they did waive their honor, the *mechilah* takes effect. If possible, it is always best to ask one's parents for explicit *mechilah*.

If a Parent Waives His Honor

6. It is not necessary for the parents to use the term *mechilah*. As long as it is clear from what they say that they waive the honor, for example, if they answer "Okay" or "As you wish," or a similar expression, it is considered *mechilah*.

7. Even though we say that if the father or mother waive their honor, it is valid, if the child nonetheless honors them, he is credited with a mitzvah, as long as his parents are pleased with the honor he shows them. However, if they get no pleasure or benefit whatsoever, then it is not a mitzvah.

8. It is up to the parent to decide how long he waives his honor. If the parent specifies that he waives a certain honor forever, one need not ever ask again for his *mechilah*. However, if one asked for a waiver only for a single instance, it does not apply to subsequent occasions.

9. A father or mother may withdraw their *mechilah*.

10. The parents should not regularly waive their right to the honor due to them, and one should not request a permanent waiver.

11. If a father wishes to serve his son, the son may accept the service from his father. However, the son should not accept it immediately; he should at first refuse. If the father himself is a *ben Torah*, the son should not accept service from him unless the father pleads very hard and the son knows for sure that his father will be pleased if the son accepts the service. If so, the son

may accept. (If the son needs the assistance of his parents, see chapter 6, paragraph 17, for guidance in how to address them.)

12. If one is sick, and one's father is near the sickbed and wants to attend to his son's needs, it seems that one may accept his father's offer even if his father is a *ben Torah*.

Chapter 10

Laws of Precedence in Honoring Parents

In parashat Toldot it says, "And Yaakov listened to his father and to his mother, and he went to Padan Aram" (Bereishit 28:7). Why doesn't the Torah say simply "to his father and mother"? Why does it add v'el, "and to his," which appears superfluous? It may be to indicate to us that in his going Yaakov fulfilled two mitzvot: honoring his father and honoring his mother. His father told him to go there to get married, and his mother told him to go there to get away from his brother, Esav. Yaakov intended to fulfill both of these: the request of his father and the request of his mother.
— *Ta'ama DiKra*

1. If one's father tells him, "Bring me a drink of water," and his mother also says, "Bring me a drink of water," even if his mother asked first, he should set aside the obligation to honor his mother and first honor his father, since both he and his mother are obligated to

honor his father. Similarly, if his father tells him to do something and his mother says not to do it, he should obey his father.

2. If one's father asks him to do something that will cause him to incur expenses that he must pay from his own pocket, and his mother tells him to do something that conflicts with his father's request, some say he may listen to whichever one he prefers, since he has no obligation to honor his father using his own money. Some say that in a case like this one must listen to his mother.

3. If one understands that his father does not want him to do a particular thing, but his father has never said so openly, and his mother asks him to do it, his mother's request takes precedence.

4. If one's mother asks him to bring her a drink of water, and his father tells him not to bring it, he should not listen to his father.

5. If one's father asks him what his mother told him, and he knows that if he tells his father the truth his father will be angry at his mother, he should not tell his father what his mother said. "It is permitted to be less than truthful for the sake of *shalom*" (*Bava Metzia* 23b).

6. If the parents are poor and they are asking for food and clothing from their children, and the children have only enough for one of the parents, the mother comes first.

7. If one's stepfather asks for a drink and one's mother asks for a drink, he should first give his mother.

Divorced Parents

8. If one's parents are divorced, and both his mother and his father asked for a drink at the same time, he can bring to whichever of them he prefers. Some say he should try to bring a drink to them both at once.

9. If one's parents are divorced and his father remarried, and both his mother and his stepmother ask for something at the same time, the honor of his mother comes before the honor of his stepmother. But if his mother tells him not to honor his stepmother out of jealousy, he need not listen to her.

10. The rule that if one's parents are divorced one may respond to whoever one wishes applies only if they both asked simultaneously. However, if one of his parents asked first, he should respond to that parent first. If one parent asked for something and the other did not, but there is something one can do for the second, the parent who asked comes first.

11. If one's parents are divorced and his father is a *talmid chacham*, the honor of his father comes ahead of the honor of his mother.

12. If one's parents are divorced and his father asks him to do something, but his mother does not want him to do it because it disturbs her greatly, or vice versa, it is

best to sit tight and not to do anything — *"Sheiv v'al ta'aseh adif."*

13. It is not proper for sons to participate in the marriage of their mother after she divorced their father.

Chapter 11

Kibbud Av Va'Em in the Context of Other Mitzvot

Why did Binyamin merit that the resting place of the Shechinah would be in his territory [in Eretz Yisrael]? It can be compared to a king who had many sons, and as they grew up each went to his place in life. The father loved the youngest [who was the last at home], and the father would eat and drink with him; the father would lean upon him when he came in and lean upon him when he went out.

That is how it was with Binyamin, who was the youngest of the children of Yaakov Avinu who founded the tribes. Yaakov Avinu used to eat and drink with him and used to lean upon him when he went out and lean upon him when he came in. HaKadosh Baruch Hu said, "The place upon which that tzaddik [Yaakov Avinu] rested his hands is where I will rest My Shechinah." That is why it says, "And He rests between his [Binyamin's] shoulders" (Devarim 33:12).

— *Yalkut Shimoni 957*

1. If one has the opportunity to do two mitzvot — *kibbud av va'em* or a different mitzvah — and he has not yet started to do either of them, which takes precedence? If the second mitzvah can only be done right away or he will lose the opportunity, but there is someone else available who can do it, he should do *kibbud av va'em*. However, if there is no one else to do the second mitzvah, then he should do that mitzvah and leave aside the honor of his parent, since both he and his parents are obligated to honor God (by doing mitzvot).

2. This rule — that he should let someone else do a mitzvah if another person is available and take care of his obligations to his father — applies only if his father is not asking him to do something for him in order that the son should not do the mitzvah; the father just wants his son to do something for him. If one's father wants him to honor him because the father specifically does not want him to do the other mitzvah, since he does not value mitzvot, one should not listen to his father.

3. If one started doing a mitzvah, and then his father asked him to do something, he should first finish doing the mitzvah he is engaged in (even if the mitzvah can be done later or it can be done by someone else). One who is engaged in a mitzvah is not obligated to do any other mitzvah at that time. Similarly, if one is engaged in *kibbud av va'em*, and suddenly another mitzvah presents itself, he need not do that other

mitzvah (even if he can only do the mitzvah at that time, and there is no one else who can do it). Some say that in the latter case he should set aside honoring his father and do the second mitzvah.

4. This law — that if one is engaged in *kibbud av va'em* and suddenly another mitzvah presents itself, he need not do that other mitzvah — applies only if his father is not obligated in that other mitzvah. If his father is also obligated to do it, he must waive his own honor to let his son fulfill the mitzvah. For example, if a father and son were together, and the son was busy doing something to honor his father, and then they came upon a lost object that should be returned, the father must waive his honor and allow his son to return the object, unless the father returns the object himself.

5. If a child is living in *chutz la'aretz* with his parents and wants to move to Eretz Yisrael to fulfill the mitzvah of living in Eretz Yisrael, but his parents need his attention (for example, if they are old and cannot do everything for themselves), the child is in a situation of being occupied with a mitzvah and so is not obligated to do another mitzvah (as explained in paragraph 3 above); therefore, he should stay with his parents. However, if one must move to Eretz Yisrael to educate his children properly, then one should do so even if it means he cannot do the mitzvah of *kibbud av va'em*. In any case, he should do whatever he can to take his parents with him to Eretz Yisrael, or he

should arrange for someone else to attend to their needs in *chutz la'aretz*. If one's parents do not need his services at that time, he may go to Eretz Yisrael, even against their wishes.

6. If a *kohen* has a *yahrtzeit* for his father or mother, and since he is leading the services he will not *duchen* (say the blessing of the *kohanim*) because there are other *kohanim* present, it is nonetheless better for him to be a *sheliach tzibbur* and lead the services than to *duchen*. In some communities, a *kohen* who is a *sheliach tzibbur* still *duchen*s, even when there are other *kohanim* present, so there is no conflict.

Kibbud Av Va'Em and Torah Study

7. Learning Torah is greater than *kibbud av va'em,* as we see from the case of Yaakov Avinu. Yaakov suffered from the sale of his son Yosef for as many years as he did not honor his parents while he was away in Charan. But the years he spent learning Torah in the House of Ever were not counted as years that he did not fulfill his obligations to his parents.

8. Learning Torah supersedes *kibbud av va'em* only when honoring one's parents interferes with one's primary growth in Torah. But if it is a question only of spending a short time honoring them, and it will not interfere with one's main learning, he must stop his learning to attend to his parents. Therefore, if a son son is sitting and learning Torah, and his parents ask him to

do something, or even if they do not ask him but he sees that they need his help and he cannot arrange for others to take care of it, he should stop learning, do what they need, and then return to his own learning.

9. The obligation to interrupt one's own learning in order to honor one's parents applies only to providing something they need for themselves, such as feeding them or another personal service. However, if they request something that is not a personal need of theirs, he is not required to perform the service if doing so would involve an interruption in his Torah learning. Therefore, if one's parents ask him to attend a family *simchah*, and doing so will interfere with his learning, he need not heed their request.

10. If one's parents want him to visit them, and they personally enjoy such visits, he must visit them due to his obligation to honor them, even if it interferes with his Torah learning. Even if they did not explicitly ask him to visit, but he knows that they want him to visit, he must visit them.

11. If one wishes to learn in a yeshivah where he is confident that he will be successful in his learning, but his parents do not want him to go there out of concern for his well-being, he need not heed their request. But if there is a choice of yeshivot, one in his city and another somewhere else, and he is unsure of his success in either yeshivah, he should listen to his parents if they tell him to study in the local yeshivah.

12. If one's father objects to his learning in a yeshivah that follows a different approach and *hashkafah* from the father's, one must do what his father wants unless it is absolutely clear to the son that without a doubt he will not succeed if he follows the approach that his father follows. In such a case, he need not listen to his father. It is best to consult with a *chacham* to determine the degree of success or lack of success that must be present before one may refuse to do what his father wants in such a case (see also chapter 8, paragraphs 33–35).

Chapter 12

Laws of Striking or Cursing a Parent

If one strikes his father or mother, he will surely be put to death.

— *Shemot* 21:15

If one curses his father or mother, he will surely be put to death.

— *Shemot* 21:17

I heard that once one of the gedolim asked one of his sons to bring him his coat, and another son brought it. He criticized that son and said, "Did I ask you? I asked your brother!" Maybe he meant that since he had asked the other son, it was not correct for that son to grab the mitzvah. And perhaps that son must pay his brother ten gold pieces.

— Rabbi Yitzchak Zilberstein, *Avnei Zikaron*

1. One who curses his father or mother, even if they are no longer alive, could be put to death by a *beit din* if he cursed them in front of witnesses and was warned

that he was committing a capital crime. This applies to women as well as men, if they are old enough to be liable for punishment.

It applies only if the curse was formulated with one of the special Names of Hashem. If the curse was formulated with a lesser Name of Hashem (a *kinui*), then he has transgressed a Torah prohibition just as one would if one cursed any member of the Jewish nation, with all that this implies. If one cursed his parent without using any Name of Hashem, he is not punished with death or with lashes, but it is still a transgression of a Torah law, and it is included in the Torah's curse "Cursed is one who disgraces his father and his mother" (*Devarim* 27:16).

2. If one strikes a parent, it is also a capital crime and one is liable to be put to death by choking. This applies if he drew blood from them. If one strikes a parent and does not draw blood, it falls under the category of the Torah prohibition against striking any Jew. Therefore, if the blow causes an insignificant amount of damage (less than the value of a *prutah* — about three-quarters of an American cent), then the striker receives lashes. Otherwise, he pays for the damages he caused.

3. Even if one's parents are absolute *resha'im* and sinners, one may not strike or curse them, but if he does so, he is not liable to punishment by *beit din*. If his parents repent and afterward he strikes or curses them, he is liable according to the laws outlined above.

Laws of Striking or Cursing a Parent

4. If one's father has a splinter, one should not take it out, because he may thereby draw blood. Someone else should take it out. But if there is no one else and his father is in pain, he may take it out.

5. If one is a nurse or a doctor, he should not draw blood or amputate a limb of a parent, even if it is to help the parent. Someone else should perform the procedure. If there is no one else and his parent is in pain, he may perform the necessary procedures as long as the parent permits it.

6. If one's father or mother is ill and needs an injection every day, and finding someone to come and give them the injection involves extensive efforts and expenses, and one is experienced in giving injections, he may give the injection to the parent himself. This applies to an injection done in a place that usually does not cause bleeding. However, if the vein must be penetrated (for example, for a blood test), then someone else should do it.

7. A child may scratch the parent's back and also shave him and cut his hair and nails.

Chapter 13

Honoring Other Relatives

Adam came into the world. Shet his son came after him. They said to Shet, "Serve your father." Shet fed him and took care of all his needs.

Shet came into the world. Enosh his son came after him. They said to Enosh, "Serve your father." Enosh fed him and took care of all his needs.

They said to Enosh, "Serve the father of your father." Enosh said to them, "I am not required to serve him."

Enosh came into the world. Keinan his son came after him. They said to Keinan, "Serve your father." Keinan fed him and took care of all his needs.

They said to Keinan, "Serve the father of your father." Keinan said to them, "I am not required to serve him."

Things proceeded in this way [for ten generations] up to Noach.

Noach came into the world. They said to Noach, "Serve your father." Noach fed him and took care of all his needs.

They said to Noach, "Serve the father of your father." Noach accepted it upon himself and fed the father

of his father and all of his fathers who were [alive] at that time. Not only that, but he went out and protested [all the bad deeds] during the 120 years until the Flood came. Therefore the Torah came and said of him to all the generations that he was a tzaddik.
— *Tanna D'Vei Eliyahu Rabbah*, ch. 16

Honoring a Stepmother or Stepfather

1. One must honor his father's wife, even if she is not his own mother, in his father's lifetime. One must also honor his mother's husband, even if he is not his own father, in his mother's lifetime. This is a Torah-based obligation.

2. Even though one must honor his stepfather and stepmother, he need not be in awe of them. Nonetheless, it is customary not to call one's stepfather or stepmother by their names, but rather to refer to them as "Mother" or "Father."

3. The honor one must show to a stepfather or stepmother is exactly the same as the honor one must show to his father or mother — except for rising. For a stepfather or stepmother one need rise only when they come within his four *amot* (eight feet or less), but for his father or mother, he must stand up when they are visible. Also, if the stepfather or stepmother ask him to do something from which they have no personal benefit, he need not honor them by doing it.

4. If one's father has waived the honor due to his wife (the stepmother), or one's mother has waived the honor due to her husband (the stepfather), it is valid and one is not obligated to honor them. Nonetheless, it is proper to honor them, unless the father has said explicitly that the children should not honor his wife (their stepmother) or the mother her husband (their stepfather). In that case, they are not allowed to honor them.

5. If one's stepfather or stepmother waived their right to honor, it is valid. But if one's mother protests that her husband (the stepfather) should be honored, or the father asks that his wife (the stepmother) be honored, he must honor them even if the stepparents have waived their right.

6. If one's father passes away, one need not honor his father's widow. But it is proper to honor her even after his father's death, and *yirei Shamayim* conduct themselves this way. This, of course, applies also to the mother's husband after her passing.

7. If one's stepfather or stepmother are *resha'im*, one need not honor them.

8. If one's father divorces his wife (the stepmother), one is no longer obligated to honor her. If she dies while married to his father, it is proper to honor her because of the honor due his father.

9. Honoring one's mother takes precedence to honoring her husband. Therefore, if one's mother asks for a

drink and her husband asks for a drink, her request takes precedence.

Honoring an Older Brother and Uncles

10. One must honor an older brother, even if he is only a half-brother from a common father or a common mother. This applies to all older brothers, not only the oldest one. Some say the obligation is rabbinical, and some say the obligation is Torah-based.

11. Just as one must honor an older brother, one must honor an older sister.

12. A sister need not honor a younger brother, even if he is the oldest of the boys.

13. If one of a set of twins is the *bechor* (male firstborn), the second one must honor him. If the older twin is not the firstborn, it is questionable whether his twin must honor him.

14. One need not honor an older brother to the full extent that one honors a parent, but one should honor him by rising and *hiddur* (a rising motion) and other expressions of honor that are appropriate for an older brother.

15. A younger brother need not show awe to his older brother. He may therefore call him by his name.

16. Some write that a younger brother should not get married before his older brother, and others write that it is not prohibited to do so.

17. If one's older brother is a *rasha*, there is no obligation to honor him.

18. An older brother may waive his right to honor, but the parents are not allowed to waive the honor due their son by a younger brother.

19. Even if the younger brother is a *talmid chacham* and greater in Torah than the older one, he must honor his older brother.

20. If one insulted and scorned his younger brother who is a *talmid chacham*, and in response the younger brother imposed a ban on the older brother (as is standard practice in such cases), this was the correct response. Since the older brother has no respect for Torah, he is not behaving as a proper member of the Jewish people and he does not deserve honor.

Honoring an Aunt or an Uncle

21. A person must honor his uncles and aunts, both on his father's side and on his mother's side. He should make a rising motion when they pass in front of him, and he should honor them in his speech. He should address them as "Uncle" or "Aunt."

    Included in honoring one's father and mother is to honor those whom his parents honor, even if they are not blood relatives. If one insults or dishonors those whom his parents honor, it is considered an insult to his parents.

Honoring One's Father-in-law and Mother-in-law

22. One must honor his father-in-law and mother-in-law. This is a rabbinic-based obligation. A woman must also honor her father-in-law and mother-in-law insofar as she is able to do so.

23. The obligation to one's in-laws means only to stand up for them when they enter one's immediate vicinity (four *amot*) until they leave and to honor them in speech. However, one need not honor them in all the other ways he must honor his parents. If one is a *talmid chacham*, he need not rise to his full height when his in-laws enter the room, but he may just make a rising motion while remaining in his place.

24. One should visit his father-in-law from time to time — for example, on holidays — as part of his obligation to honor him.

25. One need not be in awe of his father-in-law and mother-in-law, but he should not call them by their first name the way he calls everyone else. He should also not sit in their place, since this is part of honoring them.

26. The custom is to call one's father-in-law and mother-in-law using a title, such as "Reb So-and-so" or "Mr. So-and-so" or "Uncle So-and-so." Similarly, one should call one's mother-in-law "Mrs. So-and-so" or "Aunt So-and-so." Some just call their in-laws "Aunt" and "Uncle," and others call them "Father" and "Mother."

27. If one's father-in-law is visiting, one should seat him in the most honored place in the house.

28. Even though a married woman is not obligated to honor her parents (as explained in chapter 1, paragraphs 28–36), when her parents are visiting, her husband should tell or hint to his wife that she should serve her parents first. In that way he honors his father-in-law and mother-in-law, and she honors her parents. If they have done this several times, the assumption is that the husband does not mind, and she may serve her parents first on her own initiative.

29. A widower or a divorced man need not honor the parents of his deceased or ex-wife.

30. If one's father-in-law or mother-in-law is a *rasha*, one need not honor him or her.

31. If one's father-in-law or mother-in-law passed away and there is no one to say Kaddish for them, it is proper for the son-in-law to say Kaddish for them and to learn *l'ilui nishmatam* (for the merit of their souls). It is well known that the father-in-law benefits the Upper World if his son-in-law learns in his merit.

Honoring One's Grandfather and Grandmother

32. A person must honor his father's father and his mother's father. Nonetheless, the obligation to honor his father is stronger. One is also obligated to honor

his father's mother and his mother's mother. Some say he is not obligated to honor his grandparents, but one should conduct himself according to the first opinion.

33. Some say this is a rabbinic-based obligation, and others say that it is Torah-based.

34. There is no obligation to honor grandparents in all the ways that one must honor parents, but one should honor them by rising for them and speaking respectfully to them and with humility.

35. One is not obligated to be in awe of his grandparents. Nonetheless, he should not address them by their first names since this is not respectful.

36. Even if one's parents have passed away, one must still honor his grandparents.

37. If a grandparent passes away, and there is no one to say Kaddish for him, the grandson should do so.

38. If a grandparent is a *rasha*, one need not honor him.

39. Honoring a parent takes precedence to honoring a grandparent. Therefore, if a parent and a grandparent make concurrent requests, the parent comes first. However, if the requests are made when all three are present — for example, if the father and grandfather both ask one for a drink in front of each other — one should first serve the grandfather and afterward the father. But if the father objects, one should serve his father first.

Chapter 14

Honoring Parents after Their Passing

Honoring one's father and mother after their deaths is [at least] like honoring them while they are alive. This is because one who honors them while they are living has the incentive of his awe of them and the incentive of the inheritance they will leave. However, one who honors them after their deaths honors them only l'shem Shamayim.

— *Semachot 9*

❊ ❊ ❊

A son must honor his father, as it says, "Honor your father and your mother," and this is interpreted to mean...in food and drink...in his lifetime, and after he dies he must honor him even more.

— *Zohar, Bechukotai*

❊ ❊ ❊

It is proper that for his entire life a son should have his father's image before him, and the son should imagine that the father is crying bitterly from a raging fire, saying, "My son! My beloved, have mercy upon me. Save my soul from the sword; save my unique soul from the dog." And even if he thinks that his father is a complete tzaddik and that his soul is enjoying its surroundings, he should imagine that he is giving his father tasty foods that his father loves, so that his father's soul will bless him. Therefore, he should not fail even one day in his life from saying Kaddish and giving tzedakah for the soul of his parents.

— Pele Yo'etz

1. Just as one must honor his father and mother in their lifetimes, he must honor them after their passing. According to most authorities, this is a Torah-based obligation.

2. Honoring one's parents after their deaths includes doing those things that are known to bring a spiritual benefit to the souls of the departed and also to honor them in ways that are intrinsically honorable, such as referring to one's father as *"avi mori* — my father, my teacher." He should also be careful in aspects of being in awe of them, such as not referring to them by first name and heeding requests that they expressed during their lifetimes, if this does not involve a loss or interfere with the harmony of one's household.

The Laws of Kaddish and Praying for the Benefit of Their Souls

3. There is a custom to say Kaddish for one's father and mother after their passing. This custom is based on

the mitzvah of *kibbud av va'em*, since one must honor one's parents in death as in life.

4. The Kaddish that sons say for their parents is known as "*Kaddish Yatom.*" It is also sometimes called "*Kaddish Batra,*" since it is said at the end of the *tefillah*. According to the Sephardic custom, it is the Kaddish said after *Tanna D'Vei Eliyahu* and before *Aleinu*. According to the Ashkenazic custom, it is the Kaddish said after *Aleinu*.

5. It is customary that those saying Kaddish for their parents also say the Kaddish before *Hodu* at the beginning of the *tefillah,* and the Kaddish after the *Shir shel Yom* at the end of the *tefillah*. The other Kaddeishim are said only by the chazzan.

6. Kaddish D'Rabbanan is the Kaddish said after learning *Torah shebe'al peh* (Oral Torah). According to the letter of the law, anyone may say it. However, since nowadays usually only mourners say it, if one's parents object to him saying it in their lifetimes, he should heed their wishes.

7. A son may not waive a benefit that is due a departed one. Therefore, a son should not give up a right he has to lead the *tefillah* or to say Kaddish, both of which are beneficial to the soul of his father and mother. If it is a situation in which the other party will be distressed if he insists, then he may defer to another since it is assumed that his departed parents also prefer that course of action.

Honoring Parents after Their Passing

8. Whoever says Kaddish to benefit the soul of his father or mother should intend, in saying the Kaddish, to sanctify Hashem's great Name. Nonetheless, it does not detract if he also intends that his saying Kaddish should also benefit the souls of his father and mother.

9. With regard to how long one should continue saying the Mourner's Kaddish, there are three main opinions: (1) Some say Kaddish should be said only for eleven months. This is the Ashkenazic custom. (2) Some say Kaddish should be said for twelve full months. This is the usual custom of some of the Sephardic communities, including the community of Aleppo. (3) Some say he should say it twelve full months less a week. This approach has been adopted in most Sephardic communities.

10. Some say that these three approaches as to when to stop saying Kaddish are applicable only when the sons themselves are saying Kaddish and not when someone else is saying Kaddish. Someone who is hired to say Kaddish should say it for twelve full months. Others say there is no difference.

11. Some say that the rabbinical Kaddish that is said after learning from the Oral Torah and, similarly, the Kaddish that is said after *Tehillim* is said for twelve full months according to all opinions. Some say that a Kaddish that is recited after a special learning session that is for the benefit of the departed during the year of mourning for a parent should be determined ac-

cording to the opinions that were expressed with regard to the issue of when to stop saying Kaddish (see paragraph 9).

12. Some people count the eleven or twelve months with regard to saying Kaddish from the day on which the departed was buried. Others count from the day of the passing.

13. Whether the Kaddish must be said for eleven or twelve months, we count the period by the months. Even if there is an extra month in the year, we do not add a month to the time for saying Kaddish.

14. If someone knows that his father or mother were among the people cited in the *Shulchan Aruch* as being judged for twelve months, it is proper and even obligatory for him to say Kaddish for twelve full months. If one's father was a tzaddik, but nonetheless he told his son to say Kaddish for him for twelve months, the son should heed his father's wishes.

15. One who is mourning over his father or mother should lead the *tefillah* in the synagogue if he is able to do so. Leading the *tefillah* is better for the soul of the departed than saying the Mourner's Kaddish.

16. It is the Ashkenazic custom that on Shabbat and *yom tov* a mourner does not lead the services, whether during the *shivah* or during the initial thirty-day period or during the twelve-month mourning period. He also does not lead the services on Rosh HaShanah or Yom Kippur. On Rosh Chodesh, as well as on

Honoring Parents after Their Passing

Chanukah and Purim, a mourner is permitted to lead *minchah*, *ma'ariv*, or *shacharit* up to Hallel. Hallel and *mussaf* should be led by someone else. The Sephardic custom is that the mourner may lead the services even on those days and he may say *mussaf*. This is especially so if the mourner is a chazzan whose *tefillah* the community likes to hear.

17. If one does not know how to lead the entire *tefillah*, he should just lead the services at the end of the *tefillah*, from *Ashrei* and *U'Va L'Tzion*. He should especially try to lead the *tefillah* on *motza'ei Shabbat*, since that is the time when the souls are being returned to Gehinnom after resting on Shabbat. This applies to some extent to every *ma'ariv*, since the early evening is a time of the strengthening of judgment.

18. The benefits of the son saying Kaddish accrue to the parents even after the twelve-month mourning period. Therefore the mourner should try to say Kaddish every day for the rest of his life to bring merit to their souls.

19. If someone did not find out about the passing of his mother or father for many years, it is fitting and proper that he should say Kaddish for twelve months from the time that he heard about the death. This also applies to someone who is a *ba'al teshuvah* and was not religious when his parents passed away and therefore did not say Kaddish. From the day he realizes this and decides to discharge his obligation for *kibbud av va'em*

in this area, it is fitting and appropriate for him to say Kaddish for a year from that date.

20. The custom is to say Kaddish once a year on the day that his mother or father passed away (the *yahrtzeit*) and to lead all three services. The Sephardic custom is that the son starts to say Kaddish from Friday night of the Shabbat that precedes the *yahrtzeit* and continues until after *minchah* on the day of the *yahrtzeit*. When the *yahrtzeit* falls on Shabbat, he starts saying Kaddish beginning with *ma'ariv* of the preceding Shabbat.

21. If one forgot or was unexpectedly distracted from saying Kaddish on the day of the *yahrtzeit*, and he did not say Kaddish then, he should say Kaddish as soon as he remembers to do so.

22. If one is mourning for both his father and his mother, he fulfills his obligation by saying a single Kaddish for both of them.

23. A woman should not say Kaddish for her father or mother. Therefore, if someone passes away and is survived only by daughters, other relatives should say Kaddish for the deceased. If he left no relatives who can and will say Kaddish, it is permissible to arrange for another person to say Kaddish in the person's merit. It is best to pay this other person.

24. If someone was hired to say Kaddish for someone who died without leaving sons, and then his own father or mother passed away, he may continue to collect payment for saying Kaddish for the first person

Honoring Parents after Their Passing

since the Kaddish helps them both at the same time. It is not considered a slight to his parent in any way. Similarly, one who was hired to say Kaddish for one who has passed away may also take money for saying Kaddish for others. To remove any possibility of problems, he should tell the one who hires him that he will be saying Kaddish for several people who have passed away.

25. If one's mother passed away, and his father does not want him to say Kaddish because he is concerned that people might say that he, the father, has passed away and that is bad for him — according to the Rema (the authority generally followed by Ashkenazim), the father's objection is not valid. According to the Sephardic authorities, the son should listen to his father.

    The best thing is for the son to speak to his father, and perhaps ask others to speak to his father, to convince him to agree to letting his son say Kaddish for his wife. The father should not be concerned about danger to himself. On the contrary, the merit of the Kaddish will protect him as well and lengthen his days and ensure a pleasant life.

26. If one's father objects to him saying Kaddish for his mother because the father is angry at her, one should not pay attention to his objections.

27. If one's father passes away and one's mother objects and says he should not say Kaddish during her lifetime, one should not listen to her.

28. One who does not say Kaddish for his mother because his father objects (see paragraph 25) should seek other ways to benefit the soul of his departed mother, for example, by learning Torah in her *zechut* according to his ability or by giving *tzedakah* to benefit her soul.

29. Some say that a man should not say Kaddish for others during the lifetime of his parents even if they permit it. This is the accepted custom among the Ashkenazim. According to the letter of the law, if the son knows that his parents do not object, he may say Kaddish even during their lifetime.

30. If a person tells one or all of his sons not to say Kaddish for him after he dies, they should not listen to him. It makes no difference what the motive behind the father's request was — whether the father rejects the basic idea of a benefit to the soul from saying Kaddish, or he is angry at his son, or he wishes to spare him the effort.

31. One who declines to say Kaddish for his parents is considered to have insulted and degraded them.

32. Even if one's father was a *rasha* and did many *aveirot*, it is a mitzvah to say Kaddish for the benefit of his soul. Even for a father who committed suicide — which is a very serious act whose consequences are described in *Shulchan Aruch (Yoreh Dei'ah* 345) and include the stipulation that such a person not be mourned — it is proper to say Kaddish to help his soul.

33. Some say that a *mamzer* should say Kaddish for his father, and some say that he should not say Kaddish. It is preferable for him to hire someone else to say Kaddish for his father.

Customs on the *Yahrtzeit*

34. The annual anniversary of a parent's death, known as the *yahrtzeit*, is the day upon which the person departed this world. Every year, on that date, the soul of the departed is judged again in the Higher World on whether it can be raised to a higher level. For this reason, there are special customs the children practice on the day of their parents' *yahrtzeit*.

35. The *yahrtzeit* is set according to the day of death, not the day of burial. Some say that the first *yahrtzeit* is marked on the day of burial, but in subsequent years it is marked according to the day of death, and this approach has a valid basis.

36. If one does not know when his parent passed away, he should just choose a day to mark the *yahrtzeit*. If he knows the month of their passing but not the exact day, some say he should observe the last day of the month as the *yahrtzeit*. Others say that he should observe the first day of that month.

37. It is customary that on the day of a parent's *yahrtzeit*, one leads the services of all three *tefillot* if he is able. Some lead all the services on the Shabbat before the *yahrtzeit* and also say the Kaddish after *Mizmor Shir*

L'Yom HaShabbat at the beginning of Shabbat. Some only lead the services for *mussaf* on Shabbat morning.

In many places, it is customary that whoever has *yahrtzeit* in the coming week leads the services for *ma'ariv* on the *motza'ei Shabbat* preceding the *yahrtzeit*. In many Sephardic communities, one who has a *yahrtzeit* leads all the services that week up to and including the day of the *yahrtzeit*.

38. It is a mitzvah to learn Torah on the day of a parent's *yahrtzeit* and during the preceding night. Upon finishing a learning session, if there is a minyan present, he should say Kaddish and the *Hashkavah* (prayer for the departed souls).

39. If the *yahrtzeit* is on Shabbat or *yom tov*, it is best to learn Torah for the soul of the departed on that day. Some learn on the previous Thursday night or on Friday instead. Even for those who generally learn in the soul's merit on Shabbat itself, if for some reason they are unable to learn on Shabbat one year, it is preferable for them to learn before Shabbat and not to postpone the learning session to Sunday.

40. It is the custom to get *maftir* on the Shabbat preceding the *yahrtzeit*; *maftir* is preferable than the last *aliyah*. If the day of the *yahrtzeit* falls on Shabbat, some get *maftir* on the previous Shabbat, and some get *maftir* on the Shabbat of the *yahrtzeit*. the latter is the main opinion. If possible, it is good to get *maftir* on both weeks.

41. It is a nice custom to visit the graves of one's parents

Honoring Parents after Their Passing

on their *yahrtzeit* and to pray for the benefit of their souls. It is the custom in Yerushalayim to visit the cemetery on *erev Rosh Chodesh Nissan* and on *erev Rosh Chodesh Elul*, in addition to the *yahrtzeit*.

42. Some have a custom that when they go to the cemetery on the day of a parent's *yahrtzeit*, they do not visit any other graves at the same time. However, if one visits the grave of his father on the *yahrtzeit*, or another time, one should also visit the grave of his mother and say a chapter of *Tehillim* by her grave if it is not too far away. Likewise if he visits the grave of his mother.

43. If one has not visited the graves of his parents for ten years or more, it is best if he sends someone in advance to the graves of his parents to announce that he intends to visit. Then he can go to the graves himself. It is good for him to undertake to give *tzedakah* at that time for the benefit of their souls.

44. If a parent's *yahrtzeit* falls out on Shabbat, some visit the cemetery before Shabbat, and some visit it after Shabbat. The Sephardic custom is to visit the cemetery on Thursday.

45. If one is in *chutz la'aretz* and his parents are buried in Eretz Yisrael, or vice versa, he should not necessarily expend time and effort to visit their graves. Rather, he should learn extra Torah and give *tzedakah* for their souls.

46. It is a mitzvah to fast on the day his father and mother passed away. It is preferable if, the first time that he

fasts, he stipulates that he is undertaking the fast without making an oath to do so. However, if one year he cannot fast due to illness or any other legitimate reason, he must make a *hatarat nedarim,* and he should give what he normally spends on food for one day to *tzedakah.*

47. A fast on the *yahrtzeit* is like any other private fast. If one wants to fast, he should first commit to fast during *minchah* on the day preceding the fast. Then, on the day of the *yahrtzeit*, he should say *Aneinu* in the *berachah* of *Shomei'a Tefillah* of *minchah.*

48. Some *poskim* are lenient about fasting on the day of the *yahrtzeit*, especially in our days, when people are weak. As a result, the *gedolei hador* decreed that on the day of the *yahrtzeit* one should give *tzedakah* and welcome guests in the merit of the departed soul, since these are things that everyone can do. This is the custom among the chassidim. There is also a custom that after the *tefillah* the children give out cake and drinks in the merit of the departed.

49. The Rema says that one may not eat at a *seudat mitzvah* on the night of the *yahrtzeit*. Even according to the Sephardim, it is best to keep this restriction, but in case of great need, one should ask a *talmid chacham.*

50. If one has a *yahrtzeit* during the week, he should say the prayer for departed souls, known as "*Hashkavah*," on the preceding Shabbat. If the *yahrtzeit* falls out on Monday or Thursday, when we read the Torah in

Honoring Parents after Their Passing

shacharit, some say the prayer for souls on that occasion. It is also customary to say the prayer for souls at the grave.

51. In the Ashkenazic and Yemenite communities, the custom is to mention the departed person using his or her name and the name of his or her father: Ploni ben Ploni or Plonit bat Ploni. In most Sephardic communities, the custom is to mention the departed person using his name and his mother's name. Each one should follow his own custom.

52. There is no limit to how many years the *yahrtzeit* is observed. Even if the child lives one hundred years after the passing of his father or mother, he must observe the customs of the *yahrtzeit* so that his parents may rest in peace.

53. Even if the father was a famous tzaddik and *chassid,* the son must observe all the laws of the *yahrtzeit*.

Lighting a Memorial Candle

54. There is a custom to light a candle for one's father or mother. This is called a *"yahrtzeit* candle" or *"ner neshamah."* This custom is deeply rooted in holy precincts.

55. It is customary to light a candle during the seven days of mourning after a person's passing, in the room in which the person passed away. If the person did not pass away in his home, but in the hospital or some other institution, the custom is to light the candle in the person's home. Some light a candle in the house of

the departed for thirty days. It is good to light a candle in the *beit knesset* for twelve months.

56. There is a custom to light a *ner neshamah* on *erev Yom Kippur* in the *beit knesset* (to burn throughout Yom Kippur) for the benefit of the soul of the father or mother. Before lighting one should say, "I hereby light this candle in the *beit knesset* in honor of Yom Kippur *l'ilui nishmat* my father and/or mother." Some also light on *erev Rosh HaShanah* as well as on the eve of other *yamim tovim*.

57. It is customary to light a *ner neshamah* on the day of the *yahrtzeit*. Some say it is preferable to light at the grave, and some say it is preferable to light in the *beit knesset*. Before lighting, it is proper to give a little money for *tzedakah* and to say, "I hereby give *tzedakah* and light a candle *l'ilui nishmat* my father [or mother] Ploni ben Ploni. May it be God's will that this be in the merit of his [or her] soul, to raise the soul ever higher in Gan Eden."

58. It is preferable to light the *ner neshamah* using some kind of oil. If this is impossible, he may use a candle made from wax or paraffin or whatever is available. As for an electric candle, some say this also fulfills the custom, but others say that one should use an electric bulb only as a last resort.

59. The light of a *yahrtzeit* candle that is burning in the home may be used for mundane purposes (such as reading by its light). However, the light of a *yahrtzeit* candle that was lit in the *beit knesset* should not be

used for mundane purposes just like any other candle in the *beit knesset*. Some are lenient about a candle that was lit in a *beit midrash* that is not used as a *beit knesset* — its light may be used for mundane needs.

60. One should not extinguish a *yahrtzeit* candle, even if it burns longer than twenty-four hours.

61. If one forgot to light a *yahrtzeit* candle, he should donate its value to the poor.

62. One who has a *yahrtzeit* for his father or mother and also for another departed soul should light a separate candle for each one.

    If one needs to light a *yahrtzeit* candle for both his father and mother, it is proper to light a separate candle for each of them. However, if he cannot afford this, one candle for the two of them is enough.

63. It is enough to light one *yahrtzeit* candle for the benefit of the soul and in memory of a departed one, even if there are several children who are commemorating the deceased. It is good if all the children chip in to buy a single candle. However, since it is a mitzvah to donate candles (or provide electricity) so that people will have light for learning and prayer, it is obvious that the more *tzedakah* the better, so each child should light a candle independently.

64. If the *yahrtzeit* falls on Shabbat, the candle is lit on *erev Shabbat* so that it will burn on Shabbat. If one forgot to light the candle, it is permissible to ask a non-Jew to light it during twilight at the beginning of Shabbat.

65. If the *yahrtzeit* falls on *yom tov*, it is preferable to light the candle before the beginning of *yom tov*. If the candle was not lit before *yom tov*, opinions are divided. Some say that it is a candle that provides no benefit, and therefore it is not permissible to light it on *yom tov*. But some say that it is permissible to light it at night in the room in which the meal is eaten or, even better, to light it in the *beit knesset* where many will benefit. The custom is to be lenient.

Honor through Speech

66. If one says a halachah in the name of his father within the first twelve months of his father's passing, or even if he says something general in the name of his father or even mentions his father, he should not say, "My father said..."; rather, he should say, "This is what my father, *hareini kapparat mishkavo* (I am the atonement for him), said..." This, of course, applies when mentioning one's mother as well.

    After twelve months, he should say "my father, *zichro livrachah* (of blessed memory)" or "my mother *zichrah livrachah*." Some say this applies only to saying a *devar Torah* in their names but not when saying something general.

67. The previous halachah, about saying "*hareini kapparat mishkavo*" or "*zichro livrachah*," applies even if one does not mention his parents by name, but just says "Abba" or "Father" or "Ima" or "Mother."

Honoring Parents after Their Passing

68. If one prays for himself and mentions his father or mother's name when referring to himself as their child, he need not say "*hareini kapparat mishkavo.*" Similarly, if he prays for his departed parents, he should not say "*hareini kapparat mishkavam.*" When he learns for his parents, even within the first twelve months, he should say "*zichronam livrachah.*"

69. If one mentions a parent in writing within the first twelve months of his or her passing, some say it is not necessary to write "*hareini kapparat mishkavo.*" Some are strict and do write "*hareini kapparat mishkavo.*" The Rema writes that the latter is the custom.

    More than twelve months after the passing of a parent, one should write "*zichrono livrachah*" or "*alav hashalom*" when mentioning his father in writing and either "*zichronah livrachah*" or "*aleha hashalom*" for his mother, or he may use another equivalent phrase. Some are careful to say or write "*zichrono livrachah l'chayei haOlam Haba* — may his memory be a blessing for life in the World to Come."

Other Aspects of Honor after Death

70. Sponsoring *sefarim* in commemoration of departed ones do benefit those who passed away. Therefore, it is a mitzvah to give *tzedakah* for the benefit of the souls of parents and to support those who learn Torah, whether in yeshivot or other institutions that teach Torah. In this way, as well as by donating for other

holy purposes, one fulfills the mitzvah to honor one's father and mother.

71. If children wish to have a monument made for their parents rather than purchasing a very expensive gravestone, they should purchase a less expensive stone, and with the money they save they should purchase *sefarim* and donate them to a *beit midrash*. Alternately, they can set up a *chesed* fund in their parents' memory. The Torah learning and *chesed* that is done in the parents' name will bring their souls benefit and spiritual pleasure.

72. The custom many have to name children after departed parents is based on the mitzvah to honor one's father and mother (see chapter 3, where this is discussed in some detail). Similarly, if one names a *sefer* one wrote after his father or mother who passed away, he thereby fulfills the positive commandment to honor his parents, which specifically includes honoring them after their deaths.

73. Part of being careful in fulfilling the mitzvah of *kibbud av va'em* is to be careful not to change any *minhag* or tradition of one's family, even if doing so does not involve a specific prohibition or failure to fulfill an obligation.

74. The *Zohar HaKadosh* says that when there is a family *simchah*, the father and mother come from Gan Eden to participate. For this reason, there is a custom to mention the departed parents of the *chattan* and *kallah* at their *chuppah*. In some Sephardic communities, the

Honoring Parents after Their Passing

custom is to make a *Hashkavah* (say a prayer for departed ones) at the time the *chattan* is called up to the Torah. This is a proper custom.

75. One must be careful not to swear by the lives of his parents, and certainly not to swear by his father and mother's peace after their passing.

76. If one bought a burial plot for his father, but his father was later buried elsewhere, the son may be buried in the plot he originally bought for his father. Similarly, if the father bought a plot for himself but was buried elsewhere, the son may be buried in the unused plot.

77. If one's father asked that he not be eulogized, it is a mitzvah to heed his wishes. If the father said that his children should not sit *shivah,* or that they should not observe the laws of mourning for thirty days, they should not obey. However, if the father said that his children should not observe the twelve months of mourning, it is a mitzvah to heed his wishes.

78. Even though saying Kaddish and other prayers certainly helps departed parents, these are not the main thing. The important thing is that the children follow the straight and righteous path, because they thereby bring merit to their parents. A person may ask his children to pay particular attention to a specific mitzvah, and if they do what he says, it is of greater merit to his soul than Kaddish. This is a worthwhile thing to do for someone who has only daughters, since women do not say Kaddish.

Midrashim and Mussar Sayings on Kibbud Av Va'Em

The Roots of the Mitzvah

Ulla declared at the doorway of the *nasi*: What does it mean when it says, "All the kings of the earth will give praise to You, since they heard the things that You said" (*Tehillim* 138:4)? It does not say, "the thing that You said" [in singular], but, rather, "the *things* that You said." When HaKadosh Baruch Hu said, "I am Hashem your God," and then "You shall not take other gods before Me," the nations of the world said about Hashem, "He is just declaring those things that add to His own honor." But then, when He said, "Honor your father and mother" [and they saw that Hashem was concerned for others besides Himself], they went back and admitted that the first commandments were correct.

Rava said: We learn from here that "the beginning of

what You say is true" (*Tehillim* 119:160). Is it only the beginning that is true and not the end of what Hashem says? What this comes to teach is that from the beginning of what Hashem says, it is evident that the end of what He says is true.

— *Kiddushin* 31b

❈ ❈ ❈

The Rabbis learned: It says, "Honor your father and your mother" (*Shemot* 20:11), and it also says, "Honor Hashem with your money" (*Mishlei* 3:9). The Torah made the honor one must show to one's mother and father equivalent to the honor given to Hashem.

It says, "A man should be in awe of his father and his mother" (*Vayikra* 19:3), and it also says, "You should be in awe of Hashem, your God" (*Devarim* 12:20). The Torah made the awe one must have for one's mother and father equivalent to the awe of Hashem.

It says, "One who curses his father and mother will be put to death" (*Shemot* 21:17), and it says, "Each and every man who curses his God will carry his sin" (*Vayikra* 24:15). The Torah made a "blessing" given to one's mother and father equivalent to the "blessing" given to Hashem.

This equivalence cannot be drawn with regard to striking, since Hashem has no body. Similarly for the law that the father, mother, and Hashem are partners with their child.

❈ ❈ ❈

The Rabbis learned: There are three partners in [creating] every person: HaKadosh Baruch Hu, the person's father and his mother. When a person honors his parents, HaKadosh Baruch Hu says, "I consider it as if I lived among them and they honored Me."

— *Kiddushin* 30b

❈ ❈ ❈

One of the roots of this mitzvah is that a person should always recognize and show kindness to one who has done him a favor. He should not be an ingrate and ignore the good and deny the favor, for this is a very bad character trait and is despised to the extreme by Hashem and by people. One should keep in mind that his father and mother are the reason one is in the world, and therefore it is truly fitting for him to give them all the honor and all the benefit he is able to give. They brought him into the world, and they worked hard for him when he was small.

When he acquires this attitude, it will also help him to recognize the goodness of God, may He be blessed, since He is the reason for the person's existence and the existence of all his fathers up to Adam HaRishon, whom He brought into the world and to whom He supplied his needs during his lifetime. He also ensured that the person's body is whole and his makeup proper and put within him a soul that knows and can understand. Were it not for this soul that Hashem beqeathed to him, he would be like a horse or donkey that understands nothing. He should review in his thoughts how careful he should be in serving Him, may He be blessed.

— *Sefer HaChinuch*

❋ ❋ ❋

It says, "Honor your father and your mother." It is well known that the king who established a state is not seen by all his subjects every day. Even if the first generation remembers him — the generation that actually saw the king's first coming to the state and how everyone accepted his rule, and that the king built the whole country and brought them out from slavery to freedom — the generations that come later, who never experienced servitude and never saw the king entering the country, will rebel and think that the country always belonged to them and that there is no ruler above them. There is no way to avoid this foolishness other than to be subservient to one's fathers and to accept their *mussar*. The fathers will tell their children that they were slaves and that the One Master brought them to freedom and gave them their land and settled them there.

For this reason (that the rule of the king should not be forgotten throughout the land and that all the kindness of the king in taking us out from slavery to freedom would be remembered), it was necessary for the sons to subjugate themselves to their fathers and accept their *mussar*.

This is the reason for the fifth commandment, "Honor your father and your mother." It warns you about tradition, so that a person will accept the traditions of his father, since that is the main principle behind all religions. This is not possible unless one accepts the teachings of his fathers and the Rabbis.

— *Sefer HaIkarim*

❊ ❊ ❊

Both the greatness of the mitzvah of *kibbud av va'em* and the greatness of the reward it brings are explained in the *Zohar* in *parashat Yitro* (p. 93a):

"Kabeid et avicha v'et imecha" [means] to honor them with all types of honor, to make them happy with good deeds, as it says, "The father of a tzaddik will truly rejoice" (*Mishlei* 23:24), and this is honor of the father and the mother... The way one honors HaKadosh Baruch Hu, that is the way one should honor his father and mother, because they are in a partnership with HaKadosh Baruch Hu. [There are three partners in the creation of every person: HaKadosh Baruch Hu, the person's father, and his mother; his father and mother give him his body, and HaKadosh Baruch Hu gives him his soul.] And the same way one must fear HaKadosh Baruch Hu, one must fear his father and mother and honor them with all kinds of honor.

The Extent of the Obligation

Rav Ulla was asked: "How far does [the obligation of] *kibbud av va'em* go?" He answered: "Go and see what an idol worshiper who lives in Ashkelon did. His name is Dama ben Netinah.

"One time the Sages wanted to buy something from

him on which he would have made a profit of 600,000. However, the key [to the box where the object was kept] was under his father's head [and his father was sleeping], and he did not bother his father."

Rav Yehudah said in the name of Shmuel: Rabbi Eliezer was asked, "How far does [the obligation of] *kibbud av va'em* go?" He told them: "Go and see what an idol worshiper did for his father in Ashkelon. His name is Dama ben Netinah. The Sages wanted to buy a precious stone for the *efod* [of the *kohen gadol*] on which he would have made a profit of 600,000. According to Rav Kahana the profit would have been 800,000. However, the key was under his father's head [and his father was sleeping], and he did not bother him."

The next year HaKadosh Baruch Hu rewarded him: a red cow was born in his herd. The wise men of Israel came to him [to buy the red cow]. He told them, "I know that if I asked for all the money in the world, you would give it to me [because you need the red cow]. However, I only ask of you the money that I gave up previously by honoring my father..."

When Rav Dimi came, he said that one time he [Dama ben Netinah] was wearing a golden garment and sitting among the great people of Rome, and his mother came and tore it off of him and hit him on the head and spit in his face, and he did not embarrass her.

— *Kiddushin* 31a

❊ ❊ ❊

Midrashim and Mussar Sayings on Kibbud Av Va'Em

Rabbi Tarfon's mother went for a walk in her yard on Shabbat, and her sandal broke. Rabbi Tarfon went and put his hands under her feet, moving them so that she could walk on them until she reached her couch.

One time Rabbi Tarfon got sick, and the Sages came to visit him. His mother said to them, "Pray for my son Rabbi Tarfon, for he honors me too much." They said to her, "What does he do for you?" She told them the above story. They said to her, "Even if he does it a million times, he will not have reached half the *kavod* that the Torah said one should do [for one's parents]."

— *Yerushalmi, Pei'ah* 1:1

❊ ❊ ❊

Rabbi Yishmael's mother came and complained about him to the Sages. She said to them, "Shout at Yishmael, my son, who does not honor me."

The Rabbis were dismayed. They said, "Could it be that Rabbi Yishmael does not honor his parents?"

They said to her, "How does he conduct himself with you?"

She said, "When he comes back from the *beit midrash*, I want to wash his feet and drink the water, and he does not let me do it."

They said to him, "If that is her desire, that is the way to honor her."...

Rabbi Ze'eira was pained and said, "Would that I had a father and mother so that I could honor them and inherit Gan Eden." But when he heard these two stories, he said, "*Baruch Hashem* that I do not have a father and a mother. I could not do what Rabbi Tarfon did, and I could not allow what Rabbi Yishmael accepted."

❋ ❋ ❋

When he heard his mother's footsteps, Rabbi Yosef said, "I will rise for the Shechinah that is coming."

Rabbi Yochanan said, "Fortunate is he who did not see his parents, since it is impossible to completely fulfill the obligation to honor them and one will be punished over them."

Rabbi Yochanan's father died when his mother became pregnant with him, and she died right after childbirth. The same thing happened to Abayei.

— *Kiddushin* 31

❋ ❋ ❋

Rabbi Shimon ben Gamliel said: I served my father every day, but I did not serve him even one hundredth as much as Esav served his father. When I took care of my father's needs, I would often be wearing dirty clothing, and when I left home I would wear clean clothing. But Esav would serve his father only in royal clothing. Esav said, "It befits my father's dignity that I should serve him only in royal clothing."

— *Midrash Rabbah, Bereishit* 65

❋ ❋ ❋

Rabbi Avahu said, "Someone like Avimei, my son, fulfills the mitzvah of *kibbud*."

Midrashim and Mussar Sayings on Kibbud Av Va'Em

Avimei had five reliable sons in the lifetime of his father, but when Rabbi Avahu used to come and call by the door, [Avimei] used to run to the door and open it and say, "Yes, yes!" [while he was running] until he reached the door. Rashi explains that he did not let his sons go to open the door for his father, and by crying, "Yes, yes!" he was saying that he would open the door.

The *gaon* Rabbi Yosef Chaim, *zt"l*, wrote in his *sefer*, *Ben Yehoyada*:

" 'And he said, "Yes, yes!" until he reached the door' — this is difficult to understand. Why did he have to say, 'Yes, yes!' while he was going to the door? It would have been enough to say it one time to indicate that he was coming to open it.

"It seems he did this to open the eyes of people who were walking around the courtyard. Perhaps when he said yes the first time, they were busy inside and did not hear him, and when they saw him running in the courtyard they thought he was running for his own needs, to get something or for some other business that he had at the door, and then he incidentally opened the door for his father. But now that they saw him running and saying, 'Yes, yes!' the whole time, it was clear that he was doing it to honor his father.

"It also seems to me that he wanted to do the mitzvah of *kibbud* in act, word, and thought simultaneously. When he was walking, he was doing an action, and he was thinking about the mitzvah and also saying with his mouth, 'Yes, yes!' So he was fulfilling the mitzvah in thought, word, and action simultaneously."

The Reward for *Kibbud Av Va'Em*

The following things have no limit: *pei'ah, bikkurim, rei'ayon, gemilut chassadim,* and *talmud Torah.* Of the following things one eats the fruits in this world, and the principal reward remains in the World to Come: *kibbud av va'em, gemilut chassadim,* bringing peace between man and his fellow — and *talmud Torah* is equivalent to all of them.

— Mishnah, *Pei'ah* 1:1

❋ ❋ ❋

A son who honors his father may have to spend a significant amount of time on various things that he does for his parent, especially when the parent is old and needs assistance. Even though the child certainly has satisfaction from doing the mitzvah, at the same time he feels a certain discomfort from the fact that he is not free to pursue his own interests. Therefore the Torah promised that the reward for *kibbud av va'em* is "so that your days will be lengthened"; thus there is a guarantee that in return for the time that the child dedicated to his parent, HaKadosh Baruch Hu will give him additional years of life so that the loss of time will be more than balanced by his gain.

— Quoted in the name of HaRav Yosef Chaim Zonnenfeld, *zt"l*

❋ ❋ ❋

"So that your days should be long... " (*Shemot* 20:11) — I am warning you about *kibbud av va'em* so that your days will be lengthened and you will have sons and daughters. If you honor your father and mother, your children will honor you in your old age, for in the way one measures, so do others measure him. Therefore, *kibbud av va'em* is not only for the benefit of the elders who receive the honor, but also for the benefit of the child who honors them...

— Based on *Abarbanel*

❊ ❊ ❊

If you honor your father and mother, who are the source of the material part of the person and the body, which wears out and decomposes, then without a doubt you will honor your Father in Heaven who gave you your soul, the most elevated part of you which lasts forever...and therefore the reward for honor is long days. Becoming close to Hashem, Who is the fount of life, gives long life to man. If he honors his father and mother because they are the source of his material portions, then the soul, which comes from Hashem, will also give honor to its Father in Heaven, and by cleaving to Hashem it will merit long days, as it says, "And you who cleave to Hashem, your God, are all alive today" (*Devarim* 4:4).

— *Kli Yakar, Yitro*

Being Meticulous in This Mitzvah

"Honor your father and mother" is parallel [in the Ten Commandments] to the commandment "You shall not covet." This alludes to someone who thinks that only one whose father is a *talmid chacham* or a tzaddik or a very distinguished person must honor his father, but that someone who has a simple father does not need to honor him. Against this it was said, "You shall not covet," [meaning] you should not desire to fulfill the mitzvah because it brings you honor. Rather, everything comes from Hashem's Providence. This is the father you were given from Heaven. He is your father, and she is your mother. Just like a crude villager may not covet the daughter of a king, so no one is allowed to covet anything that was not given to him by Heaven.

— *Derashot* of Maharam Vorhand, *Divrei Hitorerut*

❋ ❋ ❋

You should be very careful in the mitzvah of *kibbud av va'em*. A person must fulfill all 613 mitzvot, and through *gilgulim* he will fulfill all of them. However, the mitzvah of *kibbud av va'em* must be fulfilled immediately and to the best of one's ability, since it may not be possible to fulfill it through *gilgul:* perhaps his mother and father are tzaddikim and will not come again through a *gilgul*.

— *Pardes Yosef Kedoshim*, in the name of the Arizal

The Punishment for Transgressing *Kibbud Av Va'Em*

The punishment that comes to one who causes pain to his father and mother is very great, even if he has good intentions. This is explained in the *Zohar (parashat Vayeitzei* 164b): "Even though Rachel did it [i.e., took her father's idols without saying anything] in order to uproot idol worship from her father, she was punished in that she did not raise [her son] Binyamin and she did not live at the same time as him for even a short period. This was due to the pain she caused her father, even though she had good intentions."

❈ ❈ ❈

In a *sefer mussar* (by Rabbi Y. Kaltz, ch. 5) it is written: One may feed his father delicacies and clothe him in fine clothing and lose his share in the World to Come. For example, it is common for the elderly to eat early in the morning due to their frailty. If one's father asks for food and one answers, "The sun has not yet risen! You have to get up so early to eat?" — even if he feeds his father delicacies, he loses his reward for what he did and is even banished from the World to Come since he has shamed his father and degraded him and has no consideration for his age. [Likewise] if one's father asks, "My son, how much did you spend on this article of clothing or on this food that you bought for me?" and one answers, "What do you care? I bought it and I paid for it. Don't worry about it"; or if the son answers that he paid a lot for it when he really paid very little, but just wants to give the impression that he is spending a lot on his father; or if he thinks to himself, *When will the old man die and relieve me of this expense?*; or when his aged father speaks, the son makes fun of what he says and tells others, "My father says such things — it seems that he is getting senile."

Whoever behaves this way or in similar ways, even though he feeds his father and gives him to drink of the foodstuffs of kings, and dresses him in silk and linen is banished from the World to Come.

Intent in Fulfilling the Mitzvah

My beloved sons, after I pass away, try very, very hard to behave properly in the ways of Hashem *yitbarach* so that you will not cause me, *chas v'shalom*, great pain and embarrassment in the Higher World, and in particular you should be careful about wasting time from Torah study and not concentrating on the meaning of prayers [since] prayer stands at the highest point of the world...

My beloved sons, I have a great request of you, that after my death you not cause me, *chas v'shalom*, shame and great embarrassment because your deeds are not proper, *chas v'shalom*. [In that case] not only will I not be a good interceder for you, as strong as a pillar of iron, but I will instead be cruel toward you from the Higher World, since you caused me all this shame and embarrassment in all the Higher Worlds.

However, I am certain, my beloved children, that through your pure hearts, you will certainly try very hard to make all your deeds proper, and especially with regard to constant study of the holy and unblemished Torah every time you are free of your other pursuits, even for a minute, and also with regard to *kavanah* in the holy prayers that the Anshei Knesset HaGedolah (which included several prophets) arranged for us, and also with regard to the *berachot* that we make over food and other matters, and especially in Birkat HaMazon, which is a Torah-based mitzvah.

However, your main intention in everything should be to ensure that all your deeds are proper and done for the Creator, may His Name be blessed and elevated forever. And you should also do it all in order to fulfill the positive commandment that the Creator, may His Name be blessed and elevated forever, commanded among the Ten Commandments, to honor your father and mother... and you will get a wonderful reward especially for this intention, for this is the will of the Creator, may His Name be blessed, and I am confident that you will do all this, my beloved sons.

— From the will of the *Yesod V'Shoresh HaAvodah*

❊ ❊ ❊

How can we explain what we see from time to time — children who have cast off the yoke of Heaven, and do not even fulfill the mitzvot between man and his fellow, as they are thieves and commit other financial crimes, and nonetheless they honor their fathers and mothers greatly and are even willing to make significant sacrifices to make the lives of their parents pleasant?

How is this possible? The root of *kibbud av va'em* is in the feeling of gratitude and recognition of the son for the good that his parents did for him. In general, this feeling of gratitude obligates a person to pay back people who have done him favors. However, if a person is a taker — someone who draws everything to himself implicitly [or explicitly], thinking that the whole world is there just for him and that he owns it — then he will necessarily lack gratitude. Why should he be grateful if people are only giving him what is coming to him anyway, according to his perspective? Why should he try to pay people back or in any way benefit others — even his parents?

According to the Midrash, the wicked Esav excelled in honoring his father. "Rabbi Shimon ben Gamliel said, 'All of my life I served my father. And [with all that] I did not serve him even a hundredth of the extent that the wicked Esav served his father.' "...

On the other hand, Chazal say that the wicked Esav was very corrupt and an awful person (see *Midrash Rabbah, Bereishit* 63). How do we explain this profound contradiction in his behavior?

We find an explanation in these holy words of Chazal. Canaan told his sons five things: Love each other, love stealing, love debauchery, hate your masters, and do not speak the truth (*Pesachim* 112b). How do we understand this? How does loving each other fit with theft and debauchery?

Any society of murderers and thieves must impose an internal discipline of loyalty among comrades. Individuals must be ready to sacrifice themselves for other members of their society. Does this apparent mutual love stem from *chesed*? No, all of this apparent selflessness and willingness to benefit the other stems from their love of themselves, from the lust of each and every one and his individual desire to satisfy his lusts as extensively as possible. In order to satisfy this desire using the combined powers of a large group of individuals, it is necessary to come together and impose this internal discipline. The result is that their willingness to do *chesed* with each other really comes from their desire for theft and murder.

We find something similar in the story of the Tower of Bavel. The people of that generation said, "Come let us build a city and a tower with its top in the sky, and we will make a name for ourselves, so that we are not scattered across the face of the land" (*Bereishit* 11:4). Their desire and agreement to be united was not because they intrinsically loved each other. Rather their goal was "They will not be frustrated in doing whatever they want to do" (ibid., 6).

In their case, too, their wish to indulge their desires was what brought them together. Their goal in uniting was to join against Hashem, as it were. They wanted to remove the yoke of Heaven and to live lives of material ease, as they imagined they could, without any spiritual aspect whatsoever.

So we see that the apparent love for each other and even gratitude that we see in the descendants of Canaan and in the generation of the Tower of Bavel come from a single unholy source, namely, a calculated agreement to help each other insofar as it advances their personal goal of self-indulgence.

It was from this self-centered pursuit of personal gain that Esav honored his father. The way of the world is that a father supplies the needs of his children until they are independent, and then later the son helps his father out in the latter's old age. This did not come out of simple gratitude but rather a calculation of the benefits it brought to

Esav, the son. Esav wished to serve as a role model for his own children so that when he aged, his children would help him and not just walk away. The essence of Esav's actions was giving in order to later receive and loving the other out of love of self.

This is exactly the way of all those who are takers. Their real goal is only personal pleasure. Even if they seem to throw themselves into the fulfillment enthusiastically and energetically, it is only because they see their "investment" as one that will someday pay them even greater returns. Things went so far in the case of Esav that he attended to his father in the wonderful clothing that he stole from Nimrod after murdering him.

The Torah demands an entirely different approach to gratitude in general and to *kibbud av va'em* in particular: "Do not throw stones into the well from which you drank" (*Bava Kama* 92b). We are obligated to show gratitude even to inanimate objects — even though they certainly did not go out of their way for our benefit and can in no way be said to have good intentions. Chazal taught us here that the obligation to feel gratitude has nothing to do with the giver of what we received and whether or not he had good intentions or worked hard. Gratitude is simply an obligation upon the recipient because he received something.

Thus, one who is himself a *ba'al chesed* and thoroughly infused with the desire to give whatever he has for the benefit of someone else is most able to feel the importance of even the slightest benefit that he receives, and he will want to repay good for good and even give more than he got. He will no doubt fully express his gratitude in words as well.

His heart will be full of gratitude based on the simple fact that he received something. He will not feel it necessary to determine if his benefactor worked hard for him or not or if his benefactor intended to benefit him and how he came to do what he did that benefited him.

Applying these insights to the relationship between parents and children, even if the parents derived pleasure from raising their children, this does not take away in the slightest the extreme obligation of a child to be grateful to his parents. The child received a wealth of benefits from them. They passed on the content of their own lives, and everything that the child has came through them. Is that not enough for which the child should be grateful to his parents for the rest of his life?

Chazal said: If one causes distress to his father or mother, HaKadosh Baruch Hu says, "It is a good thing that I do not live with them, for had I lived with them, they would certainly have caused Me distress" (*Kiddushin* 31a).

If one causes distress to his parents, it is a sign that he feels no gratitude toward them, since he feels that they raised him for their own personal benefit. Chazal taught us that this approach may, *chas v'shalom,* lead one to think that he need not love and honor HaKadosh Baruch Hu. He could argue: Since HaKadosh Baruch Hu created the whole world, all its creatures, their desires, and their shortcomings, it is only reasonable that he take pity on His creations and give them whatever they need. Furthermore, there is no such thing as toil and trouble on the part of HaKadosh Baruch Hu, and He is not lacking anything as a result of His creative effort. So why be grateful to Him?

This is the kind of confused and warped thinking that may occur to one who is stingy and lacking in the trait of *chesed*. He feels that he has received something only if the giver toiled and labored over what he got. He cannot appreciate the great *chesed* of Hashem *yitbarach*. As a result, he is very far from thanking Him and serving Him.

"Whoever denies recognition of the good he receives from his fellow will in the end deny the good he receives from HaKadosh Baruch Hu." Whoever lacks the full recognition and gratitude that should be felt to his fellow will also lack the ability to appreciate the good of HaKadosh Baruch Hu. It takes the same ability to recognize the benefits that a friend brings to you as it takes to recognize the *chesed* of Hashem *yitbarach*. Therefore, if one does not feel gratitude to his parents, it is appropriate that Hashem says of him, "It is a good thing that I do not live with them," because he will surely not recognize the *chesed* of Hashem *yitbarach*.

However if one's heart is fully aware of the feelings of *chesed*, he will be enlightened and will recognize that the entire creation flows from Hashem's goodness — [as it says] "He will make a world of lovingkindness" (*Tehillim* 89:3).

And he will also understand that even the fact that HaKadosh Baruch Hu made us lacking and imperfect in body and soul is really of great benefit to us since we will be recognize His trait of *chesed* when Hashem fulfills these needs. By seeing His *chesed,* we will also cleave to Hashem's *chesed*, as it says, "As He is merciful, so should you be merciful" (*Shabbat* 133b). Thereby we will serve him with a full heart, bringing us good all the time.

— *Michtav MeEliyahu*, vol. 3

Stories about Gedolei Yisrael and Kibbud Av Va'Em

The stories are brought in no special order.

It was a blustery winter night, after a big storm. The Jews returning home from the *beit midrash* of Salant suddenly noticed someone working hard on the road, digging and hoeing. They were surprised to see someone working on the road in the middle of the night, and they went over to find out what it was all about.

"What?! Isn't that Rabbeinu Zundel working over there?"

Now they were really curious as to why Rabbeinu Yosef Zundel of Salant, a distinguished disciple of the Vilna Gaon, was digging in the road in the middle of the night. He was obviously exhausted from the effort.

"Why is Rabbeinu working here at this hour?" they wondered out loud.

Rav Zundel heard them and said, "My mother passes

by here every day on her way to shul. The rain and snow that have fallen in the past few days have left the path full of puddles and mud, and that is why I am working here. I want to clean up my mother's path to the *beit knesset* so that she will have an easy walk when she goes there tomorrow."

❊ ❊ ❊

HaRav Chaim Palagi, *zt"l*, lived a long life and had tremendous prestige and honor. He was even recognized as the equivalent of a judge on the high court of Turkey, where he lived, and a royal honor guard was posted in front of his house twenty-four hours a day!

Once HaRav Palagi was asked by his students what had caused him to merit such a long life. The *rav* proceeded to list dozens of things that bring long life, and one of them was "one who takes care of his parents even if they are senile and difficult."

— Quoted in *Tuvcha Yabi'u*

❊ ❊ ❊

In the book *Toldot Adam*, written about Rav Shlomo Zalman — Reb Zalmale — of Volozhin (the brother of Rav Chaim of Volozhin), it explains that as a result of Reb Zalmale's extreme closeness to Torah and spirituality, when he needed something physical he would not ask for it explicitly but would rather hint at what he wanted by quoting a saying of Chazal that talks about that matter. For example, when it was time to eat, he would quote the saying "Rabbi Yosei said: " 'And man became a living soul' (*Bereishit* 2:7) —

the soul that I gave you: make sure it lives!" (*Ta'anit* 22).

This was the way he conducted himself with all the other needs of the body, such as drinking and sleeping — he would quote a saying of Chazal that is connected with those functions.

Rav Binyamin Ravkesh of Shklov once said that he knew about this conduct of Reb Zalmale for many years and never had any questions about it. However, once he told a great *talmid chacham* about it, a friend of Reb Zalmale. The friend said it was not true. "I am willing to have the heavens and the earth verify that the tzaddik Reb Zalmale once asked me for two pennies to buy a piece of honey cake!"

Rav Binyamin was very surprised to hear this and some time later he had the opportunity to ask Rav Chaim of Volozhin, the brother of Reb Zalmale, if it was in fact true that Reb Zalmale asked only for his bodily needs by indirectly quoting a saying of Chazal. Rav Chaim answered, "Yes, that is certainly true."

Then Rav Binyamin said that Rav So-and-so had denied that this was the case.

Even before he had finished his question, Rav Chaim asked, "Perhaps he wanted to buy a piece of honey cake?"

Rav Binyamin was surprised that Rav Chaim knew the details and replied, "Yes, but what is special about honey cake?"

Rav Chaim said, "Listen carefully to this wonderful *hanhagah*. Our honored mother told my brother, with the full force of *kibbud em*, that every day, about two hours before his main meal, he should eat a piece of honey cake (her intention was to relieve a weakness that he had). I'm sure you can easily see how this fit in with his general conduct. Since his eating this specific food is a direct fulfillment of *kibbud eim*, he asks for it explicitly and clearly. The proof for this is that you can see that every time before he eats that piece of honey cake, he learns and reviews the laws of *kibbud av va'em*."

❋ ❋ ❋

Rav Chaim Kanievsky, the nephew of the Chazon Ish and son of the Steipler Gaon, Rav Yaakov Yisrael Kanievsky, *zt"l,* said that the Chazon Ish was very careful about the mitzvah of *kibbud av va'em*. Every day he would go to visit his mother and talk to her for about half an hour. There is no doubt that the Chazon Ish, a *gadol b'Yisrael*, did not discuss with his mother the latest Torah *chiddushim* he had discovered. Rather, he chatted with her about things that interested her to make her happy.

One day he was deeply involved with his learning and apparently forgot to go to his mother. When Rebbetzin Miriam Kanievsky, *a"h,* the sister of the Chazon Ish and mother of Rav Chaim Kanievsky, visited later that day, her mother mentioned in passing that her son had not visited her that day.

When the Chazon Ish heard this from his sister, he immediately ran as fast as he could to his mother. "My mother the *tzaddeiket,*" said Rav Chaim Kanievsky, "tried to run after her brother to calm him down, but she could not catch up to him."

That is how seriously *gedolei Yisrael* take the mitzvah of *kibbud av va'em*.

— *Kol B'Ramah*, Tishrei 5760

❊ ❊ ❊

One time a young boy mentioned in passing that when he said Birkat HaMazon at home, he turned away from his mother since she did not cover her hair. The Chazon Ish said he was wrong, since according to the letter of the law it is enough to close one's eyes before a woman's uncovered hair (see *Mishnah Berurah* 75:5). The Chazon Ish he should not behave more strictly where it conflicts with *kibbud em* since turning his face might be seen as insulting to her.

— *Mevakshei Torah*

❊ ❊ ❊

The *rav* of Butchatch was a great *gaon*. He was a close *talmid* of the Kedushat Levi and of Reb Moshe Leib of Sassov, *zy"a*, and authored many works, including *Da'as Kedoshim*, *Machazei Avraham*, and *Eishel Avraham*. He wrote that before he went to visit his parents he spent thirty days learning the laws of *kibbud av va'em* and reviewing them well, so that he would be sure to know how to properly fulfill this great mitzvah.

❊ ❊ ❊

In the book *Ana Avda* (a biography of Rav Shmuel Tzvi Kowalsky, *zt"l*), it says that when Rav Shmuel Tzvi was young, before he went home during the breaks, the

Chazon Ish told him that a *bachur* who is planning to go home for *bein hazemanim* must learn the laws of *kibbud av va'em* in *Shulchan Aruch*. It is no different from what Chazal said, that thirty days before a *yom tov* one must learn and discuss the laws of that *yom tov*.

Some years later, Rav Kowalsky would tell those who studied with him that if they had not learned the laws of *kibbud av va'em* for thirty days before *bein hazemanim*, they had an increased obligation to learn those laws during *bein hazemanim* based on the *takanah* of Moshe Rabbeinu that one must learn the laws of each *chag* during the *chag*.

As a rule, the Chazon Ish warned against friction between a son and his parents and used to stress to boys that they should not display excessive piety at home. He suggested, for example, that if the son wanted to go to the *mikveh* before *tefillah*, he should say that he was doing it to refresh himself, "to cool off," as the Chazon Ish put it.

❋ ❋ ❋

HaRav Shlomo Zalman Auerbach, *zt"l*, related the following story. There was once a wonderful Jew living in Jerusalem called Reb Eliyahu ben Reb Moshe. He was always happy and greeted everyone warmly.

One day his friends and neighbors noticed something different about his mood. There was a cloud hanging over him, and it was clear that something was bothering him. Many tried to find out what had happened, but he would not say.

However, the matter did not let Reb Eliyahu rest, and he eventually unburdened himself to one of Jerusalem's great *talmidei chachamim.*

"For several nights recently I have been having the same dream. I see my father, *zt"l,* appear before me, dressed in a clean coat, white as snow — aside from one large fat stain that stands out, right on the front. My mother, *a"h,* keeps asking my father to take off the coat so that she can wash out the stain, but he answers, 'No! Only my son Eliyahu can do it, not you...'

"But I," finished Reb Eliyahu, "have no idea what to do to help my father."

Reb Eliyahu could not rest. He traveled to holy places; he traveled to the graves of tzaddikim. He prayed with effusive tears that HaKadosh Baruch Hu somehow tell him what he must do for his father.

One day it occurred to him to review his father's finances. He had already paid back all of his father's debts, as his father had asked him. But maybe there was some mistake?

When Reb Eliyahu reviewed his father's papers, he was very surprised to find a small piece of paper that had information about a small debt of his father's that had not yet been paid off but had mistakenly been put among the paid notes.

Reb Eliyahu immediately paid off the debt. That same night his father appeared again in a dream, but this time his coat was pure white, without any stain, and he was smiling.

❃ ❃ ❃

From his youth, the tzaddik HaRav Baruch Toledano, *zt"l*, was distinguished from other boys of his age group by a nobility of soul and enhanced spirituality. Even when he was quite young, his soul was already suffused with a true, pure *yirat Shamayim*. Truth was ever the light of his path, and he had a deep sensitivity for others and tried to do *chesed* for them. In particular, his *kibbud av va'em* was done with feeling and serious consideration, and it impressed all who knew him.

When he was only nine years old, the young Baruch became seriously ill. He lay in bed convulsed with pain, crying and sighing from his suffering.

Suddenly his father came in to visit him. As soon as Baruch noticed his father, he stopped crying and gritted his teeth with determination to ensure that no expression of the pain he felt would escape his lips. It truly required all of his strength to hold everything within, to ensure that his father would not see how he was suffering.

At that time, his friend Yosef Mashash was there in the room. (Rabbi Yosef grew up to be the *rav* of the Sephardic community in Haifa.) The youth was stunned to see the heroic efforts of his friend, and after Rav Baruch's father left the friend asked him, "How did you manage to remain silent? You are suffering so much!"

The nine-year-old Baruch replied, "I did not want to cause pain to Father. It is enough that I suffer. I did not want my father to suffer as well."

Another time, Rav Baruch was sitting with his

friends at a festive meal to celebrate finishing a *masechta*. As all began to enjoy the meal, they noticed that Rav Baruch did not eat anything. They asked him, "Why don't you eat? It is a *seudat mitzvah!*"

Rav Baruch replied, "I am fasting."

They pleaded with him to explain why he was fasting. He explained, "Yesterday I was with my father at the *beit din*. Suddenly, one of the litigants whom my father found at fault began arguing and protesting very vehemently that he was right. Getting excited and carried away by his feelings, that man used some strong words, and he insulted my father. I could not remain silent, and I objected to his words. My father was not happy with my protest. He was very upset that I had embarrassed that man. After I left the *beit din*, I undertook to fast in order to atone for the pain I caused my father."

❊ ❊ ❊

One time a mother and her son came in to speak with the Baba Sali, HaRav Yisrael Abu Chatzeirah, *zt"l*. The son seemed angry. His hair was long and wild. His clothing was garish. It was clear that he had been brought against his will.

When their turn came, they went in to see the tzaddik, and the *gabbai* read out the request of the mother: "I, the mother of my son, request that Rabbeinu bless him and influence him to treat his mother with respect, so that he not stumble over the mitzvah of honoring one's parents."

Both mother and son looked to the tzaddik to see

how he would react. At first he did not say anything. His face expressed a deep sorrow. Then they heard him saying, as if to himself, "Ah! If I only had a mother... If I had a mother, I would carry her on my shoulders. I would dance for joy!"

A tear rolled down the face of the great man.

Visibly moved, the son turned to his mother and said, "Mother, forgive me! I beg your forgiveness for all the distress I have caused you. Please forgive me for all the pain I have brought you."

❋ ❋ ❋

The *gaon* and *mekubal* HaRav Salman Mutsafi, *zt"l*, used to fulfill all the mitzvot with joy and enthusiasm, but the mitzvah of *kibbud av va'em* aroused in him a great awe, and he would fulfill it with special alacrity.

His son related that the way his father honored his mother, *a"h*, was outstanding. Rav Mutsafi used to designate a special place for her to sit in his house, and no one was allowed to approach her without a reason. Even though she was able to do things for herself, he would attend to her needs himself, even as the rest of his own family used to take care of his needs.

He would help her put on and take off her shoes, and he would kiss her hand. He held her and accompanied her to every place she wanted to go. He never let her wash her hands in the sink; hewould bring a large cup and bowl to where she was sitting. At mealtimes he would serve her himself, and he never let anyone else help her.

He did everything. More than anything else, one never saw him going against her will.

His mother thought very highly of him, and once, when she wanted to go stay with some of her other children in Tel Aviv and Haifa, he pleaded with her to stay with him. She answered, "Your main assistance I am saving for *Olam Haba*. I am confident that you will be of great assistance to me over there. In this world, I will go to my other children."

When his son was born, Rav Salman's mother asked him to make a festive meal the night before the brit milah, known as *"brit Yitzchak,"* and to invite the tzaddikim HaRav Efraim Cohen, *zt"l*, and HaRav Zadkah Chutzin, *zt"l*. The *rav* did not agree with the custom of celebrating with a festive meal before the brit milah, since he felt it was improper to hold a *seudah* before the mitzvah is fulfilled.

Nonetheless, he did what his mother asked, and he invited the great *rabbanim* to come to his house for a *seudah*. He said, "I am going against my own opinion in order to fulfill the mitzvah of *kibbud av va'em*."

❊ ❊ ❊

Once, when the Chazon Ish was seven years old, when the family sat down to eat, his mother noticed that her young son was not eating. "Why aren't you eating?" she asked him.

"They forgot to give me a fork," he answered.

When his mother looked at his plate, she saw he had

no meat on it. "But you don't even have any meat on your plate!" she exclaimed.

The young Avraham Yeshayahu looked at his mother sheepishly, but did not say anything. His mother understood that he had mentioned just the fork because he did not want to embarrass her by pointing out that she had forgotten entirely to give him a portion.

— *Chedvat Chaim*

❊ ❊ ❊

Rav Yitzchak Borodiansky, *shlita,* the son-in-law of Rav Shlomo Zalman Auerbach, *zt"l,* says that the efforts of his father-in-law to clarify the laws of using electricity on Shabbat (Rav Auerbach wrote one of the earliest works on the subject) stemmed from his *kibbud em.* His mother, *a"h,* needed to use a hearing aid. She refrained from using it on Shabbat because she was not sure if it was allowed and was concerned that maybe it was prohibited. When he saw how she suffered on Shabbat from not being able to use her hearing aid, her son undertook to research the entire subject and write a book about it.

— *Mevakshei Torah*

❊ ❊ ❊

One time on *erev Shabbat* Reb Eliezer of Vishnitz, *zt"l,* the author of *Damesek Eliezer,* was going over the parashah *"shenayim mikra v'echad Targum"* (reviewing the text of the parashah twice and once in Aramaic translation). As he was about to begin the last *pasuk,* his father, the author of *Ahavat Yisrael,* came in and asked him something.

He immediately stopped and answered his father.

After his father was satisfied and left, he started reviewing the whole parashah from the beginning, since the Arizal says that it is best to review the entire parashah from beginning to end without any interruptions. One of his students was watching, and he was amazed. "Certainly," he said to him, "your father would not have minded waiting for a minute until you finished reviewing the parashah. Now you will have to start from the beginning all over again."

The Damesek Eliezer turned to his student and said, "*Kibbud av va'em* is a mitzvah from the Torah itself. What value does *shenayim mikra v'echad Targum* have if I let my father wait for even a minute?"

❋ ❋ ❋

Rav Yisrael Shimon Kastelanitz, *shlita,* one of the distinguished elder Slonimer chassidim, said that Rav Mordechai Slonim, *zt"l*, told him that he once lived in Tzefat and once, on Friday night, he went for a walk with two of his friends, Reb Itche Meir Zeiger Macher and Reb Moshe Zeiger Macher. On their stroll they passed by the window of an elderly man, and they heard him singing a beautiful, sweet *niggun.* They went in to him and asked him about that wonderful melody, and he told them its story.

"I had a son," he said, "who passed away, but in his lifetime he used to honor me very much in person and with his property. He used to send me generous amounts of money, so that I lacked nothing.

Stories about Gedolei Yisrael and Kibbud Av Va'Em

"One time my son fell ill, and he sent me a message informing me of it. I went to visit him and sat by his bedside and said the entire book of *Tehillim*. Hashem, may He be blessed, accepted by prayers, and my son got up from his sickbed and became healthy again.

"Some time later he got sick again, and I went to visit him and again prayed for him. Hashem accepted my prayer, and my son recovered again.

"Some time later he got sick a third time, but by the time I got there he was already not among the living, *Rachmana litzlan*.

"Not long after, he appeared to me in a dream at night, and I saw that he was lying on a golden bed. I asked him about the bed, and he said that they made it for him out of all the coins he had sent me during his lifetime. I heard him singing a *niggun* that was pleasant and sweet. I learned that melody, and it lodged within my memory. Then my son disappeared. Since then I sing that melody that I learned and that is what you heard."

That melody is well known among the Slonimer chassidim today.

— *Kibbud Av Va'Em HaRif*

❈ ❈ ❈

One time a yeshivah student went to Rav Yaakov Kanievsky, *zt"l*, the Steipler Gaon, and told the him that the student's father had become weak and asked him to come help in his store a few hours a day. The Steipler related to him an incident that he had witnessed in Bialystok.

A widow once wrote her son several times that he should leave the yeshivah and come to help her with her *parnassah*. Rav Yozel, the Alter of Novardok, would not let the boy go. However, she kept on writing and pleading, and the boy eventually went home. In the end, he threw off the yoke of Torah entirely, went to university, and from then on he entirely ignored his mother's requests for help.

The Steipler Gaon concluded, "While he was in yeshivah, his mother could come asking for *kibbud em*. But after he threw off the yoke of Torah entirely, it was no longer possible to ask him to fulfill any mitzvah."

To the young man who had come to him for advice he concluded, "If you stop learning, you will turn out badly, and your father will not even be able to ask you to help him. It is better for you to stay in yeshivah and he will have *nachat* from you!"

After all this, he said he should still help his father, but only the minimum necessary, and he should not stop learning on a regular basis.

— *Toldot Yaakov*

❋ ❋ ❋

Rabbi S. Korach once related:

I was witness to a wonderful way of conduct that shows how one must fulfill *kibbud av va'em*.

I remember once, when there was a *seudat mitzvah* in our home, my father, *zt"l*, told me: "Go to Mori Chaim Kissar and invite him in my name to the *seudah*."

When I got to Mori Kissar he whispered to me, "You must ask my mother for permission."

I was shocked. A man who is elderly and a *talmid chacham* needs his mother's permission? But I had no choice, so I went to her and told her that my father requested that Mori Chaim come to the *seudat mitzvah* in our home. To my surprise she answered, "I do not allow it. He must rest since he is tired."

Embarrassed, I went back to him and said, "Mori, Your mother does not agree."

He whispered to me again, "I want to go. Go back and plead with her."

That is what I did, and after several pleadings and cajolings she said, "Fine. I agree. But he should not stay there a long time."

I went back to him and with speed and enthusiasm he got dressed to go. I had the impression that he was very happy, and he rushed so that his mother would not have time to change her mind.

I thought about it and I marked how far and to what age and to what extent is the obligation to honor one's mother extends.

— Rabbi S. Korach, *Mishnat Chachamim*